A Miscellaneous Lawyer

A Collection
of Humorous and
Interesting
Law Stories

D1133752

BY ROBERT C. BAXLEY

No one gets through life unscathed.
— *CRF*

AUTHOR'S NOTE

The thing is to become a master and in your old age to acquire the courage to do what children do when they know nothing.

—*Henry Miller*

In the Winter-Spring of 1998 I wrote my first book, *The Lifeguards, a Reminiscence of West Coast Beaches in the 1950's*. I sent it to several publishers, but they were not interested unless I made it into a history book plus gave them 90% of the gross sales to print and distribute the work. I was surprised at what I was told was the standard publisher-writer (new author) contract, which also included their percentage for all other sales including movie rights. I was so annoyed, I produced it myself with some excellent help in editing and production. The book turned out very well and has gone into its third printing. One thing I hadn't anticipated about my stories was the reaction of several persons in the stories and certain family members because I didn't mention my sweet Aunt Rose in the "Before I was a Lifeguard" chapter. Aunt Rose became my surrogate mother when my mother was committed to a mental hospital after a nervous breakdown. One of the persons in one of the stories, although his real name was not used, was sore for several weeks because he thought it portrayed him in a bad light. My first wife was sore because she felt my story about the rescue of the Marines made her look bad. Even though these stories were true, I felt bad about hurting the sensibilities of these persons that I liked and respected.

Finally, I have heard from several sources that some of my close friends, and not so close friends, have said: "If Baxley can do it, so can I." It is quite possible *The Lifeguards* may be responsible for a proliferation of fascinating stories.

In this work I have changed the names of many persons hoping not to annoy or embarrass them or their families by the past.

I guess this is the risk of writing a book of true stories unless no one reads it. So, if anyone is sore over their participation in these stories, accept my apology in advance and keep it to yourself.

DEDICATION

"I wonder, Mr. Tutt,
if you would be willing
to take a criminal case where
there wouldn't be any
prospect of a fee,
simply to prevent a
miscarriage of justice?"

From the 1920's into the 1940's, Arthur Train, a former Assistant District Attorney of New York County, wrote a series of stories about a lawyer named "Ephraim Tutt." These stories, published in the *Saturday Evening Post*, were so popular that American readers wanted to, and many did, believe that Tutt was real. Train further helped this myth by writing a Tutt autobiography called *Yankee Lawyer*.

Tutt always represented the underdog, a helpless person unjustly accused by some bloodthirsty prosecutor, a conniving person or corporation trying to steal his or her property. Tutt, independently wealthy, always won and never charged his downtrodden clients a fee. What a lawyer!

Arthur Train received many letters begging Tutt to take their cases. Even when told that Tutt was a fictitious person, many refused to believe Tutt didn't exist.

Early in my law career, I was introduced to this *Yankee Lawyer* by a lovely bookseller, Joe Herwig who had a used bookstore on 5th Avenue two doors west of Broadway in San Diego, California. Over my years of practicing law, I collected them and read them many times. Joe, a wonderful friend, did more for my literary education than any school, teacher or professor I ever had. Joe and his bookstore are gone now and I dedicate this work to his memory and with thanks for all the lovely hours he gave me with his books.

TABLE OF CONTENTS

ILLUSTRATIONS

BIOGRAPHY MONTAGE *by Kathleen Blavatt,* pg.131

Robert W. Conyers, Gerald Brown, Norbert Ehrenfreund, George S. Hickman , William Low, John S. Rhoades, David R. Thompson, Hugo Fisher, Joseph Alioto, Richard Goodbody, Joseph Sinclitico, Charles R. Faust, William Sommer, Al Davis.

BEFORE I WAS A LAWYER

I'm nobody! Who are you? Are you nobody too?
Then there's a pair of us don't tell!
They banish us you know.

—*Emily Dickinson*

**I have spent my whole life looking for it,
never knowing what it was.**

—Paul Newman

I was born August 20, 1929 in San Diego. I spent my early years in Mission Beach feeling secure and having a normal childhood until my parents divorced when I was five. My father split leaving my mother to support and raise me and my brother Neil, who was about two years older. It was in the middle of the depression. My father did not support us and times were tough for the Baxleys. We lived in a converted garage in Old Mission Beach on the bay side of the peninsula.

On one side of Mission Beach was the ocean and on the other Mission Bay. The ocean side is protected by a concrete sea wall built by the WPA during the depression. Between the north side of Ocean Beach and the south end of Mission Beach, the Mission Bay channel was spanned by a bridge over which the trolley, cars and foot traffic passed. Mission Bay had channels, mud flats and much vegetation which was a fish and wild life sanctuary. The bottom was alive with fish, clams and scallops.

It was in this setting, after my father had abandoned us, that Charlie Wright became the male figure in my life. Charlie was a strong, virile man in his late forties. He was a stunt man in the movies and a real hero to the local kids. He taught me how to swim using a bamboo pole with a rope attached to one end with a belt. Charlie would hook the belt around my waist and swing me in the water from the pier. When the time was right he would let loose of the rope and I was swimming. After I could swim the water became my home. I soon learned to dive and was gathering clams and fish from the bay. I had a deal with a local dentist to get him a bucket of scallops for 25 cents each Saturday. This was enough to get me to the Strand Theater in Ocean Beach for the Saturday matinee. Five cents each way for the trolley, ten cents for the ticket and five cents for a "big nut chew". I wish life had stayed that simple.

My mother wasn't up to managing two young growing boys and for several years I lived in Ranchita where I boarded with Ma Smith on her ranch. Ma took in kids from the county welfare service and living on her ranch taught me how to work. I used to think she was pretty tough on me, but I have since revised that opinion. It was the work habits I learned from her that helped mold my character.

My sweet mother did all she could to keep us going, but it finally got to her. She had a nervous breakdown and since we were poor, she was committed to the State Mental Hospital at Patton outside of San Bernardino. After that my dear Aunt Rose took over and was my caretaker until I enlisted in the Army on my 17th birthday. My mother stayed in Patton until I took her out after I finished three years in the Army Air Force. After she returned home, she did well and lived a normal life with her two sisters in Los Angeles.

After the Army I worked various jobs including selling peanuts at Lane Field at Padre baseball games until the summer of 1950 when I landed a job as a San Diego City lifeguard. While working for the lifeguards I attended San Diego Junior College and San Diego State College. I graduated from State in the spring of 1954. My major in college was drama and I appeared in plays at the junior college, state college, the Old Globe, the Coronado Playhouse and even had a small part in *Stalag 17* at the La Jolla Playhouse. *Stalag 17* was directed by Jose Ferrer and starred most of the original Broadway cast. The title role, however, was played by Aldo Ray. He was a great guy and I took him diving during the run of the play. I played the lead role in the Old Globe Christmas play and minor parts in several other Globe plays. This was about the time the Old Globe was promoting the Shakespeare Festival. To gain public support and financing, the Old Globe staged a Shakespearean Montage. I was cast in one of the scenes with Jackson Woolley and Dennis Hopper (a young, aspiring actor). I think the scene was from Henry V. Woolley was playing Henry, I was his General and Dennis a knight who was to attack Henry. Before our scene Dennis was very nervous because Dorothy McGuire, Mel Ferrer and Gregory Peck were in the audience. During the scene Dennis was supposed to pull his sword and challenge Henry to a fight. Dennis was so nervous that his hand was sweaty and when he pulled out his sword it slipped out of his hand and stuck in the floor across the stage where it quivered for some time. Jackson and I tried to keep our composure, but the audience had a great laugh. This incident didn't affect Dennis' career because he has become a well-known, highly successful actor. After trying acting for some time I decided I wasn't suited for it and went back to the beach.

While all this was going on I was still working for the City Lifeguards and assigned the midnight to 8 a.m. shift at the channel lifeguard station on the bay end of the north Mission Bay jetty. All I had to do was make sure boats did not leave or enter Mission Bay and respond to any night emergencies. There were no boats coming in or out and few other outside emergencies, so it was an ideal job for a student. During the summer I worked at Ocean Beach.

After I graduated from State College in the spring of 1954, I started to work full time at Ocean Beach. In the fifties Ocean Beach was a quiet family community. During this time I talked the Lifeguard Captain, Charles Hardy, into sending me to the first SCUBA school offered by Scripps Institute of Oceanography. After successful completion I became the first official lifeguard diver. During the same period I also worked, when off duty, as a commercial diver with two former Navy divers Jon Lindbergh and Willie Meyers. Jon was the son of Charles A. Lindbergh and had been an officer in the Underwater Demolition Teams. Willie was a former first class Navy hard hat diver.

I started law school in September 1961 at the University of San Diego graduating in May 1964.

Education is hanging around until you've caught on.

—*Robert Frost*

Robert Baxley's Law Office, the T. Hee Building 1059 10th Avenue,

Because I had done well in law school I was offered a job as a research assistant to Justice Gerald Brown on the Fourth District Court of Appeal. Justice Brown had been appointed to the court several years before direct from private practice by Governor Pat Brown (no relation). He had a brilliant mind, was a fine athlete and a wonderful human being. He taught me the art of plain writing.

Justice Gerald Brown

In the summer of 1965 I went out on my own and most of my work was appointed criminal defense. In those days San Diego did not have a public defender's office so appointments were made by the criminal law presiding judge from a list of lawyers willing to accept such assignments. As I remember the rate was $25 an hour even for capital cases. It was great training. One of my early appointments was a case involving two sailors charged with a drug-related offense. The co-defendant was represented by Pete Wilson, later San Diego's Mayor, a United States Senator and Governor of California. Pete did an outstanding job and both young men were found not guilty.

> ROBERT C. BAXLEY
> MISCELLANEOUS LAWYER
>
> 1059 TENTH AVENUE
> SAN DIEGO, CALIFORNIA 92101
>
> BUS (619) 236-1144

As my practice developed I started getting some good clients and interesting cases. In each of the cases, even the serious, something funny happened. This work deals with some of the more interesting cases, humorous aspects of them and some trips I took to keep my perspective on life.

In 1992 Governor Wilson appointed me to the San Diego Superior Court where I served until May 1998 when I retired due to a stroke I had several months before.

I had a wonderful time as a lawyer and I believe I helped many people through their legal riptides. As Sterling Hayden observed in his autobiography the *Wanderer,* I wouldn't change places with anyone. And to all lawyers...Hail! Not Farewell.

THE CHART HOUSE

*Buzzy Bent (far left),
John Callahan (third from left)
and Ron Smith (front)*

Buzzy Bent at the Wedge

In July 1961 the Chart House Restaurant opened in Aspen, Colorado. Alfred E. (Buzzy) Bent and Joey Cabell started the restaurant at the foot of "Little Nell" on an investment of $2,500 each. Buzzy, who grew up in La Jolla, was a well-known surfer who became an officer in the Navy Underwater Demolition Teams. He left the Navy in 1958 and built surfboards at a shop on Midway Drive in San Diego until he left to go skiing in Aspen. I met Buzzy in the early fifties when we surfed at the same beaches and dove for lobster and abalone together. He was handsome, blond, muscular and an exceptional water man.

Joey, a tall handsome Hawaiian, was one of the world's great surfers. Like Buzzy, Joey worked nights as a waiter in an Aspen restaurant so he could ski during the day. These two combined to start the first Chart House Restaurant. After opening a second Chart House in Newport Beach, they decided to go different ways in the development of new Chart Houses. Joey, more laid back, wanted to go slower. Buzzy, more ambitious, wanted to involve his friend, a fellow Naval Officer named Ron Smith and his younger brother PG.

The two went their separate ways; based on a verbal understanding they would keep their joint interests in the Aspen and Newport Beach restaurants. Joey would have the Hawaiian Islands to develop and Buzzy, California.

The Plane Wreck

In December 1965, the Shelter Island Chart House opened for business. The new group included Buzzy, Ron and PG, They had a verbal understanding that as soon as Shelter Island became successful, a second Chart House would be developed. Buzzy would own two thirds of each restaurant, PG would manage and own a third interest in Shelter Island, and Ron would manage and own a third interest in the next restaurant.

By this time I had graduated from Law School, had been admitted to practice law and was now asked to represent Buzzy and the Chart Houses.

I had been urging Buzzy to get their business agreements in writing. Up to this point, the only written evidence of their agreement was a $50,000 key man insurance policy on each of their lives, with the proceeds to be paid to the heirs of the deceased partner's interest in the restaurant.

Some time after Shelter Island opened and the money started rolling in, Buzzy and PG purchased an old World War II two seater AT-6 Texan trainer.

The plans for development took a dramatic change on July 12, 1966 when PG, with a friend, crashed the plane in the ocean in about 90 feet of water in front of Windansea Beach in La Jolla, killing them both. One of the first divers on the scene was Jim Stewart. Jim was a scientist at Scripps Institute of Oceanography and a member of the Bottom Scratchers (the first organized skin diving club in the United States and a diving friend of mine.) Shortly after Jim hit the bottom and found the wreckage, several Navy frogmen appeared at the wreck scene. The bodies were removed from the wreck and taken to Quivera Basin in Mission Bay, then flown to the Coast Guard Station next to the San Diego Airport. Pat Goddard, an employee of the Shelter Island Chart House, learned of the accident from Ron Smith, who had already identified PG and the passenger, and had called me to meet him at the Coast Guard Station. When I arrived, I had not yet learned that Ron had already made the identification.

Several days after the crash, I told Ron that we should dive to the wreck and verify that the controls were operative in both seats, which meant it would be impossible to tell who was at the controls at the time of the tragedy. I got in touch with Jim Stewart and asked him to come with us to the site and dive with us. Jim agreed and the next day we left from Mission Bay in a barge with our scuba equipment. We quickly located the wreck because it was still emitting oil. We anchored off the oil slick and headed for the bottom. We found the plane and determined that the stick was still intact in both seats. Jim was a witness to this evidence. The issue never arose because the heirs of the passenger never made a claim.

The Coronado Chart House.

After PG's death, Buzzy and Ron took my advice and incorporated the business. Buzzy owned two-thirds and Ron one-third of the stock. There were three directors: Buzzy, Ron and me. They selected me because Buzzy and Ron didn't want to show favoritism to any current employee. Buzzy was president, Ron vice-president and I was elected secretary. The accountant for the business, Bill Cole, became the treasurer. The first new Chart House was in Coronado. On the bay side of the Hotel Del Coronado was a historic old boathouse, about fifty feet from the land, resting on wooden pilings. It was owned by the City but leased to the Hotel Del. At certain times in the year when the tide was at its highest, the bottom floor was covered with seawater. Larry Lawrence, who controlled the Hotel Del corporation, wanted to lease it on a "what you see is what you get" basis. Buzzy and Ron didn't have a problem with the building itself but the pilings presented a different risk. The City Attorney for Coronado was Richard Goodbody, who had an office across the hall from mine in the U.S. National Bank building. I had coffee with him most weekday mornings at 7 a.m. Goodbody was not only a wonderful lawyer but also a wonderful person. The younger lawyer friends called him "Uncle Rich" and he was always there with time and advice for

Richard Goodbody

us. When I mentioned to Uncle Rich that Chart House was thinking of leasing the boathouse, he told me that he didn't think the city would grant a permit to operate a restaurant there because of the pilings. I passed the information to Ron and we decided to check it out. One late afternoon we drove over to the site with our scuba gear and ice picks and entered the water. All the pilings were rotten and would never stand the weight of a restaurant. When we got into the negotiation for the lease, we had a plan. We knew Lawrence would be difficult to deal with. We had agreed to the rent and duration of the lease, but the other terms had not been discussed. So when we started hammering out the other terms I started objecting to most of the tough terms favoring the landlord. This discussion went on for some time. Lawrence was getting angry and seemed about to pound his shoe on the desk, so I said ok, we would agree to the terms in dispute, but in exchange we wanted the landlord to guarantee the structural integrity of the building *and the pilings*. He agreed and we had our lease.

When we applied for our permits, the City told us "not without replacing the pilings." Lawrence was very angry but Chart House had him. This clause saved the Chart House about $150,000. The building was picked up off the water by a crane, new pilings were placed next to the shore, the tops of which stood several feet higher than the highest tide line and then the building was set back down on the new pilings. For this tip, Uncle Rich would have never had to pay for a meal at the Coronado Chart House. He never took advantage of this because he felt he was just doing his duty as the Coronado City Attorney.

Another incident with Lawrence occurred during the remodeling of the building. Chart House did their own remodeling and decoration in those days and during the course of the restoration, a minor fire happened on an upper floor. As part of the restoration, this fire damage was repaired. Unknown to us at the time, Lawrence made a $20,000 fire damage claim and was paid by his insurance carrier. I was the agent for service of process for the corporation and I was served with a complaint for indemnification by Lawrence's insurance company. Lawrence thought he could put one over on his insurance company and collect for damage he hadn't sustained. I called his lawyer and told him about the suit and said if we had to defend this lawsuit we would cross complain against Lawrence for fraud. The suit was immediately dismissed. I learned several years later, that after my call which accused Lawrence of fraud, he contacted Buzzy and Ron and tried to get them to fire me as their attorney. He accused me of being prejudiced against Jews. If I had known about it at the time I would have sued Lawrence for intentional interference with my business relations with Buzzy and Ron. They were right not to tell me.

WEIRDO

Illustrated by Charles R. Faust

A dog is a lion in his own lane.
—Hindu Proverb

Buzzy Bent acquired a small dog named Weirdo during his travels. The dog got his name because of his looks. Weirdo had long hair, a long body, short legs, a long turned up tail and tongue. He was definitely a "poi" dog (Hawaiian for unknown lineage). One weekday morning I received a telephone call from Buzzy, who sounded quite distressed, saying he needed to see me right away. I had not yet met Weirdo! About thirty minutes later Buzzy showed up at my office at 10th and C Street, San Diego.

When Buzzy arrived at the T. Hee Building with his girlfriend and Weirdo, he was shown to my office on the second floor. Buzzy was visibly upset. He put Weirdo on my desk and Weirdo waddled across and licked my cheek. Who wouldn't like Weirdo after that greeting? I asked Buzzy what the problem was and he handed me a letter. It was from the senior partner in a law firm, with offices in La Jolla, New York and other foreign countries. I picked it up and read:

Dear Mr. Bent,

This firm represents John Doe, the United States Postal carrier that delivers mail to your home. Last Tuesday, he was attacked by your dog and severely injured while delivering mail to your residence.
California Civil Code, Section 3340 provides:

The owner of any dog is liable for the damage suffered by any person who is bitten by the dog on private property if such person is lawfully on private property. A United States Postal carrier is lawfully on private property when delivering the United States mail.

Unless you contact this office immediately to settle this claim, suit will be brought against you for the serious personal injuries, emotional distress and for punitive damages as allowed by law!

Very sincerely yours,
V.I.P. Lawyer

It turned out Buzzy wasn't really worried about the threat of a lawsuit or having to pay money. He was upset that someone had accused Weirdo of doing something wrong. I managed to calm Buzzy (neither the girlfriend nor Weirdo was bothered) and told him I would take care of the matter.

When Buzzy left, I called the insurance carrier for the Chart House who also had the personal liability insurance for Buzzy. I told the agent about the letter and he said to send it on and he would take care of it. So off went the letter.

However, I was burning over the insolent tone of the letter with its threats so I decided to write a reply. My letter read:

Dear V.I.P. Lawyer,

Weirdo's master, no his friend, Mr. Bent, has given me your letter in which you accuse Weirdo of causing serious injury to your client and your claim for damages. A lawyer of your stature and vast experience must know that there are always two sides to every controversy.
I have thoroughly discussed this matter with Weirdo who gives a completely different version of the incident. Weirdo tells me that he was peacefully sunning in his yard when a funny looking man, wearing funny looking clothes, came into Weirdo's yard. Weirdo asked him what he wanted, but the man didn't understand Weirdo and kicked at Weirdo. When this happened, Weirdo bit him in self-defense.
California Law provides it is lawful for a person (dog) who is being attacked to use reasonable force to defend himself from such attack. (Bartosh v. Benning (1967) 251 Cal. App. 2d 378, 383-386).
Is not Weirdo entitled to the same standard of protection?
No need to remind a lawyer of your experience, now that Weirdo is represented by a lawyer, to have no direct communication with Weirdo. All further contact must come through me as Weirdo's lawyer.

Sincerely,
Robert C. Baxley
Miscellaneous Lawyer

I never heard from V.I.P. Lawyer again, but I learned he reported me to the State Bar Ethics Committee. Much later, I received a call from the lawyer in charge of ethics for the State Bar for the San Diego area. He asked me what V.I.P. Lawyer's complaint was about. I told him the story and sent him the correspondence. I heard he had a good laugh and ended his investigation. I suspect if V.I.P. Lawyer was around at the time of my application to become a judge I would have gotten pretty low marks.

ELDRIDGE CLEAVER

Cover of *Soul on Ice*

Toward the end of 1975, I got a call from a former law student I taught at the University of San Diego Law School, about going to the Federal Metropolitan Correction Center to talk to Eldridge Cleaver. He had recently returned to the United States, under a protective agreement with the United States Government. Eldridge was to be held at MCC until he was transferred to Oakland, California to stand trial for his participation in the famous Black Panther/Oakland Police shoot out which had occurred some years before.

In that case Eldridge had jumped bail and became a political refugee in those countries that did not have extradition treaties with the United States for the crimes for which he was charged in California. He grew tired of their governments and wanted to come home to face the consequence.

I met with Eldridge at the Federal Jail and we had a long discussion about his case. He asked me and I agreed to represent him in the Oakland charges. After a couple of weeks, he was flown to Oakland in a small plane and put in the Oakland Jail. During his time in San Diego, the media was anxious to interview him. I advised him against it and since Cleaver mistrusted the media, he refused all interviews.

After he returned to Oakland he was bombarded with lawyers wanting to take his case. Since they had free access to the jail, and because Cleaver wanted to talk and could get out of his cell to the more spacious lawyer visiting rooms, he saw everyone that asked. I advised him against such visits without success. Just before Cleaver's first court appearance, I received a call from the West Coast editor of *Time* magazine with a request to interview Eldridge. I discussed this with Eldridge and he agreed to meet with the reporter. The arrangement with *Time* was that I would be present and there would be no discussion of the facts surrounding the pending criminal charges.

To clear the way, I called the officer in charge of the jail to tell him I was coming with the *Time* reporter. I was told the reporter could not be admitted without a Court Order.

I went to the Presiding Judge of the Oakland Superior Court, who told me he didn't have the authority to order the Sheriff to let the reporter into the jail.

I went back to the Sheriff, told him what the Judge said and he repeated that the reporter could not enter without a court order.

What a catch twenty-two! I told the Sheriff we were coming on Thursday at 3 p.m. and if the reporter couldn't come in with me, we were going to hold a press conference on the steps of the jail.

We arrived and had no trouble getting in to see Eldridge. The reporter, a handsome man wearing a gray pinstriped three-piece suit, looked like he just stepped out of a Wall Street ad. True to his promise, only unrelated matters were discussed. Eldridge and *Time's* reporter spent several hours discussing world affairs and politics of the third world countries where Cleaver had spent the last several years. It was a political history lesson for me. Toward the end of the interview, the reporter asked Eldridge, "Why did you come back to California to face these charges?"

Cleaver replied, "Look around you. There is no other country where I was, where a prisoner, charged with a serious crime, could talk to the press with his lawyer present."

On the plane back to Los Angeles I had a long talk with the reporter who was impressed with Cleaver's political knowledge. I asked if he would send me a copy of his story when it was printed. He said he would, but the story never came. I suspect the interview was scrapped because it was favorable to Cleaver.

Before Cleaver's first court appearance I asked him to autograph a copy of *Soul On Ice* On this copy he wrote:

"For Bax, in the Attorneys' room of the Alameda County Jail, on the eve of our first court appearance. What shall we see when, hence, we look back upon this day? I'm nervous.
Eldridge"
1/8/76

Shortly after this Cleaver changed lawyers to a Boston attorney who agreed to represent him without charge. Eldridge's criminal problems got resolved. He later ran for President of the United States, became a preacher and died alone, as all of us will, in May, 1998 at age 62.

DOCTOR FOX

Pettis Norman

Dr. Fox was a tall, handsome man and looked like a medical doctor should look. He was the long time team physician for the Chicago Bears and had kept that position because he did what the coaches wanted: treating players to go back in the game, not necessarily getting them well.

Pettis Norman was a star tight end for the Dallas Cowboys who had been traded to the Chargers toward the end of his career. He had bad knees, which were concealed from the Chargers, when he was traded here. The Chargers soon learned of his condition, so he was given cortisone and painkiller injections to keep him playing. The painkillers took away the pain, the cortisone lubricated the joint and Pettis continued to play until his knee was ruined.

After the season Pettis, who was the player representative for the Chargers, went to Chicago for a player's conference. While in Chicago his knee became swollen and he went to see Dr. Fox. The NFL had a policy that if a player had a football related problem and was in a city with an NFL team, the player was supposed to go to the team doctor for that NFL team. Dr. Fox examined Pettis, gave him some medicine and sent him on his way. Fox followed this visit with a letter to Dr. Woodward, the Chargers' team physician.

Playing with an injured knee had ended Pettis' playing career.

I filed a lawsuit for him and during the course of that action I obtained his medical records from Dr. Woodward. In those records, I found the Fox letter to Woodward that reported his findings and treatment. The last sentence of the Fox letter said,

"I think Pettis has been doing too much too soon."

Because of this sentence, I suspected Fox might be a good witness for Pettis' trial. Since Fox lived in Chicago it was not possible to force him to testify at a trial in San Diego. My option was to take his deposition to use at the trial to bring out his opinion. His deposition could be taken in Chicago but that was a legally complicated option, or in California which was more practical. I knew the Bears were playing the Rams in Los Angeles so I persuaded Fox to have his deposition taken in Los Angeles when he was there with the Bears.

The deposition was set the Saturday before the Rams-Bears game in the hotel room of Dr. Fox. The room was full of lawyers representing the various parties. Fox was annoyed at having to go through the procedure and it was evident that he felt his time was too valuable to be wasted on such trivia. The deposition went fairly smoothly for about 45 minutes. I had obtained his file at the start and intended to finish my questioning by asking if he was critical of Woodward because Pettis was "doing too much too soon." In looking through his file I noticed that the same letter in his file had been altered, eliminating the damaging phrase. I marked the letter to Woodward as an exhibit and asked him if that was the letter he wrote and sent to Woodward. He said it was. I next asked if he didn't form the opinion that Pettis was doing too much too soon. His face got red and with a raised voice denied that sentiment! I then produced the letter from Woodward's file with Fox's signature, showed it to him and asked him to explain why the letter in his file was different from the one in Woodward's records. Fox's face got even redder. Yelling, he ran and locked himself in the bathroom. While still on the record, I shouted for him to come out so we could finish his deposition. He started yelling at me that he would not come out and that he was going to sue me.

That's how Dr. Fox's deposition ended. Unfortunately, it didn't help in the case against Woodward because the real letter was in his file.

Norman's case was tried twice. The first time, the jury found for Woodward. The Trial Judge granted a new trial because one of the jurors was overheard remarking to another juror about Pettis' green shoes. That juror said: "This must be the day for niggers to wear green shoes." The retrial didn't fare any better because one of the treating doctors from Dallas changed his testimony. I suspected the medical profession's conspiracy of silence was at work.

HANSEN SURFBOARDS

Don Hansen

He was 19 when he joined the Army and came to California from South Dakota. Tall and muscular, he looked like he came out of a surfer movie. It didn't take him long to find the ocean. A natural, he took to the water and became an excellent surfer. After the service, he started making surfboards and it wasn't long before he had his own surf shop in southern California in Encinitas. In those days, Gordon Clark had developed a formula for foam and the molds to produce the blanks used by all shapers to make the finished product. It wasn't long before he had a corner on the market and if you didn't buy from Clark, you didn't make surfboards.

Don had been to Clark's factory and learned that he made concrete forms in which he poured the foam to make the blanks. The molds were simple and functional. Clark would not sell the liquid or divulge his formula so that others could make their own blanks. Hansen decided Clark's control of the market was bad for business. He went to Dupont and had the chemists make a compound that would work in his own molds patterned after the forms he had seen at Clark's factory. All of a sudden, Clark had lost a big buyer of blanks. He didn't want others to follow, so he filed a lawsuit in San Diego seeking to restrain Hansen from making his own blanks.

Hansen hired me to represent him. I knew that the best part of Clark's suit was no good because it was based on the supposition that Hansen stole his chemical formula. The success of the Clark suit depended upon the argument that the molds were protected as a trade secret.

The law was clear that unless Clark had kept the molds secret he would lose. The case was assigned to Judge Joseph Kilgarif for a hearing on the injunction. Judge Kilgarif was one of the brightest and respected judges on the San Diego Superior Court.

Clark was represented by a fancy attorney from Newport Beach who reeked with confidence in his Brook's Brothers, three-piece pinstriped suit. With his opening statement, I learned that he believed Hansen was using Clark's chemical formula to make the blanks, in addition to copying the molds used to pour the foam. As the evidence unfolded, he was surprised to learn the foam was manufactured and purchased from Dupont, so the case came down to whether the molds were protected as trade secrets. Undaunted, Clark pushed on, using the theory that the concrete molds were protected as trade secrets.

After Clark finished his presentation, I started calling witnesses to prove that he had not kept the molds secret. First came Hansen who testified that Clark had showed him the molds and they were so simple that he made his from this viewing. Next came George from a surf shop in Pacific Beach. When George took the stand I asked him who he was and what he did. Next, I pointed to Clark at the counsel table next to his fancy lawyer and asked him if he knew Mr. Clark. He looked over to where I was pointing and asked, "Do you mean Grubby?"

I allowed, "The very same" and from then on in the trial I never referred to Clark by any name other than "Grubby." For my last witness I called an old surfer, Don Oakey, who was also an engineer. I asked if Grubby had ever shown him the molds. He said he had seen them once when Clark showed him his plant. I asked Oakey if he could draw the plan of the mold from that one visit. He allowed he could and then went to the board and drew a perfect drawing of the mold. Judge Kilgarif ruled in Hansen's favor but was glad to be rid of me and my beach friends.

I think of this case every time I walk into my garage and look at the beautiful "Hansen" long board he made me as a bonus.

ANNIE

Illustration by Ray Blavatt

In the second half of the sixties there was a major riot at Watts in Los Angeles. During and after this event the San Diego Police were afraid that there might be a similar riot in San Diego. The blacks in south San Diego planned a sympathetic demonstration in a small park in southeast San Diego called *Ocean Park*. Law enforcement was ready! On the scheduled day a large number of blacks gathered at the park. With this the police marched in and arrested several hundred blacks and charged them with a number of criminal violations such as unlawful assembly, riot, attempted riot and battery on a police officer. The assembly was nipped in the bud before it got started. More than 200 persons were arrested. Among those was Annie.

She was 18 years old, weighed about 190 pounds and had long black hair in dreadlocks. She was charged with inciting a riot and resisting arrest, both misdemeanors. Most of those arrested were charged with similar crimes. The Presiding Judge of the Municipal Court assigned these cases to Judge Charles M. Snell for trial. Judge Snell was a large man with a good sense of humor and was known to tip the bottle during the day. The City Attorney's office, in charge of prosecuting misdemeanors within the San Diego City limits, assigned one deputy to handle all these cases, one after the other. This prosecutor somewhat resembled the leading character in Frankenstein's movies. He was smart and well prepared.

Annie was about the third defendant to go to trial in front of Judge Snell. The first two had been convicted in short order and by this time the prosecutor had the evidence down pat.

Jury selection was difficult because most prospective jurors knew about the incident because of the wide media coverage and the impact of the Watts' riots. Of those prospective jurors who denied knowledge of the *Ocean Park* incident or Watts' riots either had their heads buried in the sand or were not being truthful in their answers. Because of this it took longer to select a jury than normal. There were many other cases stacked up and the Judge wanted to get on with it. Well, after a full day of jury selection we finally got a jury and were ready to start the evidence the next day. The morning of the second day of trial the prosecutor made his opening statement, which was pretty polished by this time. Annie was seated next to me at counsel table and her mother was in the audience. Her mother was a very large black woman in her early fifties with long red hair the strands of which looked like quarter inch hemp line. During the trial she frequently fell asleep and snored so loudly the bailiff had to wake her.

In presenting his case the prosecutor took two entire days in setting the scene. By the end of the second day I was sick of hearing about big black cars driving around the park and the "gathering storm." We finally got through setting the stage and a young, handsome, white police officer was called to the stand. He was dressed in his fresh uniform and made an excellent appearance. The prosecutor again set the scene and after about an hour of general questions finally asked him if he had arrested Annie. He said he had and then was asked the circumstances surrounding her arrest. He said when he first saw her she was standing on the corner yelling and swearing. He was then asked what he said to her and what she said to him. He related that he told her to "disperse in the name of the sovereign." There was an early California Supreme Court decision that held to be guilty of the crime of failure to disperse, those magic words had to be uttered. This had its origins in English Common Law and carried over into California law. When he said he told her this, I thought to myself, "You lying bastard." I suspected he learned these magic words from the prosecutors. He was then asked what happened next. To which he replied, "She swore at me." The prosecutor was not satisfied with just "She swore at me" and persisted in asking him to say exactly what she said. At this point the officer said he had a wife and small child at home and it was so bad he didn't wish to repeat the words. However the prosecutor insisted and the officer finally said, "She called me an M. F." I glanced at the jury and it didn't seem to register. When I cross-examined the officer I did not go into that part of his testimony.

On the third day of trial it finally came the turn of the defense. I waived an opening statement and put my only witness, Annie, on the stand. I had asked her in private if she had sworn at the police officer and she assured me that she had not. I told her when we got to that part of her testimony about swearing at the policeman she should look directly at the jury and give her answer. I got to that point in relatively short order and said, "Annie, I want you to look right at this jury when you give your answer to this question. Annie, you were here in court when that police officer said you swore at him? Did you swear at him?"

Annie looked straight at the jury and said, "No, Mr. Baxley. I didn't call that pig no mother fucker!"

I lost my breath and wanted to dive under counsel's table. When this happened her mother was still snoring and the judge and the jury were laughing so hard we had to take a recess.

The jury found Annie "Not Guilty". The prosecutor left in a huff and the judge started the next case. That was the last I saw of Annie or her mother.

BOB MITINGER

Robert Mitinger & Joesph Sinclitico

Imet him when he started law school in the fall of 1963. I was headed into my final year and he was just starting. He was 6' 4", weighed 235 lbs. and was as solid as a rock. He had been an All-American end from Penn State and was a number one draft choice of the San Diego Chargers of the then American Football League. His father, a well-known Pennsylvania lawyer, prepared his contract which had a "no cut-no trade" clause. He was a sensation his first year in the league. He started law school at the University of San Diego after the football season ended. We met there and became friends. His name was Bob Mittinger.

At the time, the Chargers were playing in Balboa Stadium at San Diego High School, a few blocks from downtown San Diego. In his second season, in December 1964, the Chargers hosted the Denver Bronco's at Balboa Stadium. He invited me, General George Hickman (Dean of the Law School) and Professor Joe Sinclitico (a law professor) to sit on the sidelines with the Charger players. It was a very important game and very few fans were permitted to sit on the bench with all the players.

Toward the middle of the third quarter, the Charger's starting halfback, Paul Lowe, ran an end sweep toward the direction where we were seated. I was next to Professor Sinclitico and on his right was General Hickman. As Paul rounded the corner, Denver linebacker, Wahoo McDaniels, made a flying tackle toward Lowe. He missed. I saw him in the air headed toward us. I grabbed Professor Sincilitico and pulled him to the left. Wahoo missed us but hit General Hickman knocking him "ass-over-tea kettle" breaking several of his ribs. Bob was on the bench at the time and as they carried the General off on a stretcher we both thought, "There goes law school!"

Well we both made it, but the General didn't go to any more football games.

Much later, after I had been practicing law, Bob got into a contract dispute with the Chargers and they had to pay off his contract. This led to my first legal encounter with Sid Gilman who in those days was coach and general manager. The Chargers cut Bob and paid him the remaining money due on his contract. They refused, however, to give him his two tickets to each home game. A letter from me got Bob the tickets, but the coach had the last laugh because they were in the bleachers behind a post. The seats were never used.

THE PAWN SHOP SHOOTOUT

Allen Brown

Wile I was still in law school, Robert Page Anderson was given the death penalty for killing a pawnbroker during a robbery in downtown San Diego. It was a sensational crime and a sensational trial. Anderson committed the robbery and murder in broad daylight, a few blocks south of Broadway on Fifth Avenue. During the ensuing gun battle with thousands of people watching, a spectator died of a heart attack. Anderson was captured after being shot at close range with a shotgun fired by San Diego Police Sergeant Allen Brown who entered the building toward the end of the firefight. As Brown approached the area where Anderson was hiding, Brown fired two blasts through a door and then saw Anderson with a gun in his hand. Brown fired at close range hitting Anderson in the left arm with the first shot. As Anderson spun around from the force of the hit, Brown fired a second shot hitting Anderson in the right arm. As Anderson spun back, Brown fired the third shot hitting Anderson in the abdomen. These blasts should have killed Anderson, but he was rushed to County Hospital and with heroic medical efforts, his life was saved.

When he was brought to trial both arms were shriveled and disfigured and he was still oozing at his stomach as a result of the shotgun blast.

At his first trial he was convicted of first-degree murder, three counts of attempted murder, first-degree robbery and sentenced to death. In California, in such cases, there are two trials. The first is the guilt phase; the second is the penalty phase. There is an automatic appeal to the California Supreme Court when a person is sentenced to death. On the first appeal the California Supreme Court affirmed the convictions of the crimes, but reversed the sentence of death and ordered a new trial on the issue of life or death. This happened in 1966 (People v. Anderson, 66 Cal. 2d 633).

By this time I had graduated from law school and was in private practice.

The lawyer who represented Anderson in the first trial didn't want to handle the second penalty trial and I was appointed to represent him.

The case came to trial in San Diego before Judge Robert W. Conyers in Department 12. The District Attorney assigned chief deputy Robert Thomas to handle the trial. Thomas had handled the first trial and was a very able, down-to-earth prosecutor.

Judge Robert W. Conyers

Although the jury was only deciding life or death, it was necessary to conduct the entire trial. Usually the same jury that hears the guilt trial hears the penalty trial so it is not necessary to present all the facts surrounding the crime and defenses presented in the guilt trial. Thus, this new jury had to hear everything even though they were only deciding life or death.

The trial started with jury selection. Judge Conyers was one of the most respected and liked judges on the San Diego Bench. He was tough, fair and had a sense of humor. In a criminal trial the defense lawyer questions the prospective jurors before the prosecutor. After I finished my questions, Thomas took over. In those days the District Attorney's Office kept track of every juror who had served on a criminal case. Most of the jurors on the Anderson panel had prior experience so Thomas had a lot of advanced knowledge about those prospective jurors. He was an earthy and very effective examiner. Toward the end of his examination he started to question a grandmother type seated in the front row next to the witness box. It was obvious he knew a lot about the lady. Toward the end of his questions he asked her, "Can you give this black man a fair trial?"

She responded, "Yes Mr. Thomas."

He then looked at me and said to her, "Will you listen to this young lawyer?"

She replied again, "Yes Mr. Thomas!"

Thomas then said, "By the same token, can you give the People of California a fair trial?" She gushed, "Oh, yes Mr. Thomas!"

With this answer, Thomas reached over the rail of the jury box and put his hand on her shoulder and said, "God Bless your heart!"

I just about fell off my chair. As soon as I recovered my composure I asked to approach the bench and complained bitterly to the Judge about this conduct. The judge told Thomas to watch himself but that is as far as he went.

The trial proceeded and Thomas was working the facts and jury like a finely tuned violin. I did not call any witnesses and it was time for final argument.

When it came my turn to argue, I pulled all stops to try to save Anderson from a death sentence. At one point in my argument I quoted Portia's speech from the Merchant of Venice, "The quality of mercy is not strained. It droppeth as the gentle rain from heaven Upon the place beneath: it is twice blest..."

With that statement an older male juror in the back row of the jury box turned his head and held his nose and went "Phew!"

That was the last time I ever quoted Shakespeare in a jury trial!

The jury again imposed the death penalty. However, the California Supreme Court, in a opinion written by the Chief Judge Donald Wright, reversed this decision holding the California death penalty statute as written, unconstitutional under the United States Constitution (People v. Anderson (1972) 6 Cal. 3d 880).

I did not handle the appeal, but I often remarked that I was responsible for having the death penalty, as it existed, ruled unconstitutional, adding, "If I had not lost the case it would still be in existence!"

JIM

Illustration by Ray Blavatt

Trouble rain on many already wet.
—*Charlie Chan*

He was about fifteen when I met him. I had three daughters and Jim used to hang around our house where we lived on Sunset Cliffs in a big house across from the ocean. We saw a lot of Jim. He was a skinny kid with a large head of curly greasy hair from working under cars. Jim wasn't allowed to sit on the upholstered furniture because of this. Jim talked a lot about surfing big waves, but nobody saw him in the water when the surf was up. His bragging didn't matter because he was a good kid.

I hadn't seen Jim for several months, until one Monday morning at about 8:30 a.m., I ran into him seated in the San Diego Municipal Court Presiding Department. The courtroom was crowded with people waiting to be assigned to a trial department to hear their cases. As I walked into the courtroom toward the bench, I heard a voice call out, "Mr. Bax". I looked over and saw Jim. I stopped and asked him why he was there. He told me he was fighting a ticket for littering the freeway. I told him I had to go upstairs to the Superior Court for a few minutes and when his case was assigned to a department for trial to go there and tell the clerk I was his lawyer and would be right there.

When I finished my business upstairs I came back to Municipal Presiding and learned he had been assigned to Judge Frank Nottbusch for trial. Nottbusch was a large, red-faced Judge who had been a star football player at San Diego State College in the thirties. He had been on the Municipal Court bench for many years and was known to be a heavy drinker. His face was always flushed and his nose always red. Nevertheless, he was a kind man with a good sense of justice and was liked by the lawyers. In those days the Presiding Judge assigned several cases each day to various trial departments. Some of these cases included traffic violations, which the judge would hear before the longer matters.

I got to Nottbusch's department later than I had planned. When I walked in, his clerk said she was glad I was there and that the judge was sore because of the delay in his calendar. The City Prosecutor was a new, young lawyer anxious to establish a reputation. He greeted me by saying I was in for it because the Judge was "mad as hell" because I was late. Judge Nottbusch took the bench with robes flowing and called the case. The police officer that wrote the ticket was mad because he felt Jim was wasting his time and Jim was frightened because he thought the judge was mad and I still hadn't had a chance to talk to Jim to find out what happened.

The Prosecutor called the officer who testified that he and his partner were following a speeding truck headed toward the beach on I-8 when he saw someone throw a bag from the passenger's side when the police put on the red light and siren. The bag was never recovered but the clear implication from was it contained some sort of illegal substance. Jim was given a ticket for littering and the driver for speeding. After the prosecutor finished I cross-examined the officer in detail, believing I convinced Judge Nottbusch that the officer couldn't have seen what he described. The prosecutor rested and I moved for a dismissal on the grounds the People hadn't proven a case against Jim. The Judge in an exasperated tone said "Denied. Call your witness!" I asked for a recess. The judge in an irritated tone asked why I need one. I told him I had just taken over the representation of the defendant and needed a chance to discuss the facts with him. This didn't please the Judge, but he gave me five minutes. I took Jim outside to the hall and asked him what happened. He denied throwing anything out of the truck. I told him that I was going to ask him about the incident and when I got to the part about throwing anything out of the truck I wanted him to look at the Judge when he give his answer. The trial resumed and I called Jim as my only witness. In a couple of minutes I was at the key question and said to Jim, "Jim, I want you to look at this fine Judge when you give your answer to this question, and I want to tell you that he can tell a liar in a heart beat. Jim, did you throw anything from that truck?"

Jim was magnificent! He looked straight at Judge Nottbusch and said, "No your honor. I didn't throw anything from that truck!"

Judge Nottbusch had heard enough! He said, "Not guilty" and

left the bench.

As he left the courtroom the startled Prosecutor jumped to his feet and was yelling he hadn't cross-examined the defendant. By this time Judge Nottbusch had left. As the startled Prosecutor was asking the clerk what happened, I grabbed Jim and we left the courtroom. Out in the hall Jim was just as confused as the Prosecutor and asked me what happened. I told Jim he won. Jim looked at me in wonder and said, "Mr. Bax, I knew you were a good lawyer but I didn't know you were that good."

Judge Nottbusch retired from the bench and then passed on in 1978.

I didn't charge Jim a legal fee for this "brilliant" court work and we remained pals over the years.

JULES

Illustration by Charles R. Faust & Bill Noonan

He was a slight, nervous Jewish man in his early thirties. Jules was a high school teacher and a real klutz in every sense of the word. He came to me when his wife left him and their two young children for another man who was more sexually attractive. During the divorce Jules planned to take his two children to visit his parents in the Midwest. He intended to drive across country and a friend suggested he carry a small hand gun in the car for protection. Unfortunately, he took this advise and bought a twenty two caliber automatic from a pawn shop and some ammunition. This was the first gun Jules had ever handled and he took it home intending to carry it in his car when he drove across country.

The night before he planned to leave, his wife came over to say goodbye to her children. After seeing the children and they were put to bed Jules showed her the gun and she asked him how it worked. They sat side by side on the couch and she took the gun and tried to click the trigger. Nothing happened, so she asked Jules what was wrong. Jules took the gun in his right hand. She was seated to his right. Jules held the gun up put his finger on safety and clicked off. As this was happening she looked around the barrel. He pulled the trigger. The gun went off killing her instantly. Jules called the police who arrested him and he was charged with murdering his wife. Eventually the case came to trial and was assigned to Department 12 before San Diego Superior Court Judge Robert W. Conyers. Conyers a former FBI agent was smart and fair and above all let the lawyers try their cases. We could not have had a better judge.

The prosecutor assigned to try the case for the People was thin, wiry and very intense and was a member of the same Synagogue as Jules, but to my knowledge, had never met him. A jury of mostly women was selected. The Prosecutor believed they would not like Jules for shooting his wife. I felt Jules would gain sympathy when they learned she dropped him for another man and left him with their children.

Interestingly, the dead wife's father agreed to come from Canada to be a character witness for Jules. I figured he believed his son-in-law was a good father and not capable of murder. He also knew if Jules was convicted, he and his wife, who were in their late sixties, would wind up as caretakers of the two small children. Just before the father-in-law was scheduled to testify, the Prosecutor got him aside in the hall and tried to talk him out of testifying. This so angered the old man that his testimony became even stronger.

I also called the Rabbi from Jules' Synagogue as a witness for Jules' non-violent and truthful character. The Prosecutor, who had been at odds with the Rabbi, could not resist cross examining the Rabbi and went on the attack. The Judge looked at me, expecting me to object, but I had faith in the Rabbi to handle the situation. He did not disappoint me. Toward the end of his cross examination of the Rabbi, the Prosecutor, with his voice rising almost to a scream, asked the Rabbi, how can you testify for a man who killed his wife. Judge Conyers looked at me, and I shook my head, indicating I was not going to object. The Rabbi looked calmly at the Prosecutor and replied, "I'm here because I believe Jules is morally incapable of committing murder."

The Prosecutor looked stunned and then asked the judge to strike the answer.

Judge Conyers looked at him and with a smile denied his motion.

We concluded the evidence and began closing argument. In a criminal case, since the Prosecution has the burden of proof he went first. Then the defense argues and the Prosecutor closes.

During the Prosecutor's opening he had prepared his argument in a note book and as he finished a page he would rip out the page, crumple it and throw it on the floor at his feet. I noticed that the jury was distracted by all the ripping, crumpling and throwing the pages on the floor. After he finished, he left all the pages on the floor where I was to argue. I asked the Judge if he would have the Prosecutor clean up his mess before I start. The Judge agreed and ordered him to clean up his mess.

The whole theory of the defense was accidental death-that the wife put her head in harms way. I had three big charts drawn to illustrate how this occurred. I pinned these charts to the wall above and behind me. They were just barely attached and I prayed they would not fall during my closing. I made it and with relief sat down.

The Prosecutor could not contain himself and jumped to his feet and loudly started his rebuttal argument. The first thing he did was to pick up a pointer and yell about the theory that "She turned her head toward the gun.", he struck the charts with the pointer and they all fell down on his head. The jury broke into laughter and I began to have a good feeling about the result. After the Prosecutor finished, the Judge instructed the jury and they were sent to deliberate. About four hours later they came back with a verdict of "Not Guilty!" Shortly after this trial the Prosecutor left the District Attorney's office and went into private practice.

THE FAUST(IAN) LETTER

Great Red-eyed Draftsman
Faustus Prismacolorus

Illustrated by Bill Noonan

He who looks only at heaven may easily break his nose on earth.

(Czech proverb)

Charles R. Faust, I met him in late 1969 at a party given by a mutual friend. He is a tall raw boned, muscular man who looked like he came out of an early western. He has the strongest hands of anyone I ever met. Until he retired several years ago, he was the designer for the San Diego Zoo and Wild Animal Park. He is also a remarkable artist, well known for his sand sculpture, water colors and pencil drawings. Upon meeting we became immediate friends. During the evening after drinks he told me about Smucke!

Some years before, John Smucke, who was a well known developer of mobile home parks, hired Charlie to draw a proposed mobile home park with drawings of large sculptures of animals throughout the park he was trying to develop. Charlie did the drawings and sent Smucke a bill for $250. The project was never built so Smucke refused to pay Charlie's bill. Charlie repeatedly demanded payment without success. Finally, he called Smucke and asked him why he hadn't been paid. Smucke told him his drawing wasn't any good and that's why he hadn't paid. To Charlie this was as bad as if he had called his sister a prostitute. Charlie told John he was coming down to collect. John said for him to come ahead because he would have "his boys" give Charlie a licking he would never forget. Charlie was even angrier for the threat, and now that he had a lawyer he wanted to sue the bastard. I told Charlie that a lawsuit was a waste of time because he had waited too long to sue and explained the Statute of Limitations. I could see he was disappointed so I told him I would write Smucke a letter and we would see what happened.

The next day I wrote:

Dear Mr. Smucke,

I represent Charles Faust who has told me that some years ago, you commissioned him to do a drawing of a proposed project. His work was not conditional on the success of the financing of the project. He has repeatedly billed you for this work and you have unreasonably refused to pay.

While I realize you can avoid payment because of the technical defense of the statute of limitations, the moral obligation to pay still exists! This is to advise you that unless payment, with accumulated interest is not made within ten days you will never go to heaven!

Sincerely,
Robert C. Baxley
Miscellaneous Lawyer

About two weeks later, I received a call from David R. Thompson, his lawyer (now a Judge on the U.S. Court of Appeals) telling me that Smucke was completely un-nerved. He asked me what my letter was about. I learned from David that Smucke was very superstitious. I told David the story and he laughed and said if Faust could guarantee that Smucke would go to heaven, he (Thompson) would pay the bill.

Smucke never paid and it is very much in doubt which direction he went when he passed on.

David R. Thompson

TOM

Bad alibi like dead fish-cannot stand test of time.
—Charlie Chan

He stood over six feet, weighed about 160 pounds, was muscular and spoke with a southern accent. He had grown up in Florida and wound up in San Diego via the Marines. He stayed on after a dishonorable discharge. As a child he had a serious disorder. He liked to torture animals. One of his favorite pastimes as a teenager was to catch cats and throw them off bridges into the channels headed toward the ocean.

I met him when I was appointed to represent him on charges of two counts of first degree murder where the Prosecutor was seeking the death penalty. These charges arose out of the deaths of a man and woman in Ocean Beach. The man, about 35, and the woman about 29 lived on West Point Loma Boulevard, about a block from the beach. Their bodies had been discovered about a week after their deaths. Both had been stabbed and the medical report indicated, at the time of their deaths, they were heavily under the influence of drugs. A neighbor said Tom had been the last person seen coming out of their apartment.

An all points bulletin led to Tom's arrest in Florida. He was taken into custody by the Miami police. He waived extradition and was picked up by the San Diego Police to bring back to San Diego for trial. While being transported, Tom asked one of the policemen whether California still had the death penalty.

The case was assigned to Judge William Low for trial. In my conversations with Tom, he told me he didn't do it. He said he was in Pacific Beach at the time, asleep on the beach.

The overwhelming evidence presented by the Prosecutor showed he had been there doing dope with the couple up to the time of their deaths.

I was faced with a tough decision. My client had no witness to verify his alibi and the circumstantial evidence showed he was there and killed the man and woman while under the influence of drugs. Tom took the stand and

Judge William Low denied killing the man and woman. I called several expert witnesses to establish that even though Tom committed the killings he was so under the influence of drugs that he could not form the specific intent to premeditate. I hoped if the jury did not believe his alibi, they would find him guilty of a lesser degree of murder, thus avoiding the death penalty.

At one point in the trial the Prosecutor asked a question to which I objected. Judge Low called us to approach the bench. After hearing my argument and ruling on the objection, before we started back to our seats, the judge motioned me to come closer, then said, "Mr. Baxley your fly is open."

Without hesitation, I said, "Thank you your honor, we have enough corpses in this trial already."

The judge laughed so hard we had to take a recess.

Tom was found guilty of one count of first degree murder and one count of second degree murder. On appeal the District Court of Appeal reduced the first degree murder to second so the death penalty was avoided. Tom was lucky and the case illustrated the well known belief that if the defense can show the victims deserved what they got, the jury is more likely to be lenient.

IT'S MY CAT

Illustrated by Charles R. Faust

It would have made a cat laugh.
(Planche: The cat and the frog)

Being a Miscellaneous Lawyer I handled divorce cases.

When I started practicing law in 1965 it was called divorce. Grounds in those times included irreconcilable differences and adultery. In cases where a lot of assets were involved private investigators were hired to get the goods on errant spouses. The desirability of proving either of these grounds was so the Court could make an uneven distribution of the community property to punish the wrongdoer. In 1970 California adopted "no fault" concept for termination of marriage .

It eliminated much of the bitterness in the fight for assets. I was glad, because I never liked the spying associated with contested divorces.

In the early seventies a nurse (I'll call Betty) had made an appointment to discuss getting out of her marriage to a much older man, a psychologist (I'll call him Dr. Pudgy). She was a handsome woman in her late thirties. He was in his mid-fifties, pudgy, out of shape and shorter than Betty. The Doctor wore an obvious toupee and was the type of person who always looked rumpled even in a freshly pressed suit. They had been married about three years and had not acquired much property during their marriage. She told me she just wanted out! I thought this would be a snap, but I hadn't understood the emotional factor, namely the good Doctor didn't want to let her go. He was so set on keeping her that he hired a well known, high priced divorce lawyer to fight the case.

First, he didn't want her to have spousal support or any property acquired during their marriage. Betty could care less about property or support. When he learned this, he said he wanted the cat.

"That does it! No way is he getting my cat."

He had found a nerve. I told her it was going to be expensive to go to court over the cat.

She said, "I don't care what it cost. If that son-of-a-bitch thinks he's going to get my cat, he can go straight to hell in a hand basket." In asking for her cat the good doctor had awakened a spark that filled my client with resolve.

The day for trial arrived and down to the court house we went to be assigned to a trial department to decide the case, mostly, who got the cat. While waiting for the case to start, I spoke with the Doctor's attorney and told him the judge was really going to be sore over taking court time over a cat, and urged him to have a "come-to-Jesus-meeting" with his client.

He went back to Doctor Pudgy and I watched them in the corner arguing. After about ten minutes his lawyer came back and said, "OK, she can keep the cat." We went into court and put a stipulation on the record and left.

My client was happy to have him out of her life, but her now ex was very bitter and angry about losing her.

I thought the case was over and I could get on to other matters. Wrong! About two weeks later I got a letter from the Doctor's lawyer, saying his client was emotionally upset at the time of the settlement and was thinking about making a motion to set it aside. However, he was willing to forgo this, if the ex-wife was willing to permit him reasonable visitation with the cat.

I called Betty and read her the letter. She told me,

"Tell that son-of-a-bitch to go to hell! He was never going to see my cat or me again!"

I told her I would pass this message on and wrote this letter to his lawyer:

Dear Clyde,

I have discussed your client's request for reasonable visitation with the cat and my client is negative to this suggestion. She feels this request is simply a means to have contact with her, and has nothing to do with any emotional attachment to the cat.

However, in the spirit of reasonableness, if your client is willing to pay for an analysis of the parties and the cat, by a board certified cat psychologist, and the report indicates it will not be harmful to the cat, my client is willing to give his request serious consideration.

Very sincerely yours,

Robert C. Baxley

Nothing more was heard from the lawyer or his client. Much later when I ran into the good Doctor's lawyer at a bar dinner he told me the Doctor had a fit, called me a dirty bastard for playing light with his feelings and wanted to sue me for emotional distress. He was sobered by the cost of bringing such suit. That was the last I heard about him, her or the cat.

THE OLD MAN

Judge William Mahedy

He was white, in his late seventies, short and weighed about 150 pounds. The Old Man was charged with murder for shooting his abusive son-in-law. The problem was he shot the son-in-law five times, three in the front and two in the back.

I was appointed to represent him and the case was assigned to Judge William Mahedy for trial. At the trial, we took the position that the Old Man shot his son-in-law in self defense during a violent beating.

I talked to the Old Man a lot and believed his story. The problem was the number of shots. My expert would testify the first shots spun the son-in-law around that was why the last two hit in the back.

Judge Mahedy was a large, hot tempered Irish, no nonsense Judge. He got loud and threatening if you disagreed with him. The Old Man told me about numerous beatings by the son-in-law. In addition to the abuse on the Old Man, the son-in-law bragged about killing a prison guard and seriously injuring other people. To establish the Old Man shot because he feared for his own life, which would make it self defense, I had prepared a written brief on self defense to give to the Judge if the Prosecution objected.

The time came for the Old Man to testify and after some preliminaries, I asked him if the son-in-law had ever physically abused him. The Prosecutor arose and in a most indignant tone, objected to this line of questioning. I told the Judge prior acts of violence by the decedent showed the state of mind of the defendant, and was admissible to show the Old Man acted in self defense. Judge Mahedy looked annoyed, but overruled the objection. I took the Old Man through a series of acts where his son-in-law had kicked, beaten and threatened to kill the him. The prosecutor didn't like this testimony and was becoming increasingly agitated! I hammered this home for quite awhile.

After finishing questions of the direct acts of violence by the son-in-law against the Old Man I started into a line of questions involved the son-in-law bragging to the Old Man about acts of violence against others. At this the Prosecutor had more than he could endure and he jumped to his feet objected. Judge Mahedy sustained the objection. I had anticipated this and had prepared a written brief on the subject. I replied in my most academic tone, "This evidence is also admissible to show state of mind." I asked to give the written brief to the Judge. Judge Mahedy, or Wild Bill as he was known by the trial lawyers, went into a rage. His face got red and he yelled "Baxley, I said sustained! Now get on with it!"

I was stunned by his outburst and backed off the subject. About this time we took a recess for lunch. When we came back to court about 1:45 p.m. I was still steaming! I told the court clerk that I wanted to see the Judge in Chambers with the reporter present before the jury was seated. In a few minutes the Prosecutor and I were shown into Mahedy's chambers. The Prosecutor didn't know why I insisted on seeing the Judge. When we got settled I said to the Judge, "I have been appointed to represent this Old Man and I'm doing the best I know how to see he gets a fair trial. Your ruling about the evidence of acts of violence against others was wrong! You should have considered the law allowing such evidence." With my voice raised I concluded, "If you want some patsy to defend this poor bastard you should relieve me and appoint another lawyer!"

I looked around and the court clerk and reporter's faces were ashen. The Prosecutor smiled as though he believed I was on my way to jail. I then looked back as the Judge smiled and said, "Aw, cool down Bax."

I was completely disarmed! Judge Mahedy loved a good fight. The trial continued. The Old Man was found not guilty. It has been said the best defense in a murder trial is to show the victim got exactly what he deserved. It was true in the Old Man's case. The prosecutor didn't speak to me much after that trial, but Judge Mahedy and I became good friends until his death in 1984.

MY TATTOO

Robert Baxley Diving

Photographed by Richard Grigg

Sometime it crosses my mind that the things I write
here are nothing other than images that sailors tattoo
on their skins.

—*George Seferis*

Ihave already told you about Charlie Faust. Over the years he has given me art for Christmas, birthdays and just because he liked me. He is one of my close friends. In the early seventies, I was at his shop in Ocean Beach and I told him that I was so proud of our friendship and his art that I wished he would design a tattoo that I could put on my body in recognition of our friendship. To humor me, never dreaming I was serious, he drew a pelican in flight. I had a friend, a Navy Captain named Buck, and asked him to find out who was the best tattoo artist in the Pacific Fleet.

Several days later Buck called and reported his sources told him it was "Iwo Jima Eddie". He said he had a place in National City near the Naval Facility. Iwo didn't have a telephone so I drove to his place one week day. I was dressed in my business suit. I found his place and knocked on the door. The door opened a crack and a voice asked me to state my business. I asked him if he was Iwo Jima Eddie. When the voice said yes, I told him I heard he was the best tattoo artist in the Pacific Fleet and I was interested in a tattoo.

With this, the door opened and a small skinny man in his seventies let me in. Iwo had tattoos over his entire visible body and I suspected over the covered parts also. He took off his shirt and showed why he was called "Iwo Jima". His back had a magnificent tattoo of the famous flag raising on that South Pacific island.

I showed him the Faust drawing of the pelican and asked him if he could duplicate it on my rear end. The drawing had a circle with a c in the center (a common law copyright) and he said he could do it but he wouldn't. I asked him why? He said it was copyrighted! A tattoo artist with ethics! I asked him for a pair of scissors. He handed them to me and I cut the copyright sign from the drawing. This satisfied Iwo who said, "Now it's all right."

He explained he had to do a transparency of the pelican to transfer to my body and that would take a few days. He asked me where I wanted it placed and I told him the spot on my left butt.

I asked him how much this was going to cost, and thinking he had a pigeon he told me $35. I said, "What?" Thinking he was going to lose me, he reduced the price to $30.00. When I again said, "What?" Iwo knocked another five dollars off and said that was as low as he was going! I told him, "No way." Iwo thought I was a pretty tough negotiator until I said I wasn't going to pay less than $100.00 for a tattoo of a drawing by such a famous artist! Taken completely by surprise, Iwo beamed and said he would do it and give me a lifetime guarantee. We shook hands to seal the deal and off I went.

About two weeks later I returned and the tattoo was installed in the chosen place.

I went off to Hawaii to dive for black coral with my friend Ricky Grigg and nearly didn't return with my tattoo. Ricky took me to a spot off Lahina on Maui called "Stone Wall." The depth was over 200 feet. We agreed before entering the water that when we had seven minutes bottom time (counted from the time the diver leaves the surface to the time the diver starts up) or 1000 pounds of air left in our tank, we would start toward the surface. We anchored his boat over the spot and descended down the anchor line. Ricky's wife, Carol, stayed in the boat. The water was clear and warm but the current on the bottom was strong. The plan was to gather coral trees and tie them to the anchor line to be hauled to the surface after we had decompressed. I hadn't counted on the amount of air I was consuming by hauling the trees to the anchor line. After attaching a second tree I looked at my air gauge and saw I was down to 100 pounds. I started for the surface and at about 100 feet I had sucked my tank dry. I knew I could not come up too fast and that I had to exhale. Somehow I made it to the surface. Carol handed me another tank and I went back to 20 feet and started to decompress. I was very lucky not to have been killed.

After I returned to San Diego I didn't see Charlie for several days. The next time I saw him I showed my tattoo and, although somewhat dismayed, we had a good laugh. Charlie made the mistake of telling his wife, Nancy, about the event and she didn't speak to either of us for several days.

Designed by Charles R. Faust

You may be wondering how all of this relates to my law practice. Well, every time I got a nasty letter from another lawyer, when I wrote a reply, at the bottom of my letter under my signature I would insert "kmp/rcb". The lawyer would never get it, but I felt better by expressing my feelings.

If Governor Wilson had known about my tattoo, he probably would have had reservations about appointing me as a Superior Court Judge. Well, Pete it's too late now.

THE BRUSH FIRE
NEAR THE NUDIST CAMP

John T. Holt

He was a volunteer fireman charged with arson arising from a brush fire at the Swallows Nudist Camp in east San Diego. The State Department of Forestry had long suspected him of setting various fires around the County and had a lookout posted on a hill overlooking the Swallows Nudist Camp.

The suspect, a volunteer fireman, was believed to be a "Vanity Pyromaniac." A pyromaniac was a person that gets a sexual charge from setting fires, and a vanity pyromaniac is a person that gets a double hit–setting the fire and then helping to put it out.

Jim was tall and wiry in his early twenties. He and his girl friend lived at the Swallows Nudist Camp. She was small and wiry like Jim and was a dancer at a topless bar nearby named The Match Box. I don't remember how they came to me but when I was hired his soul mate paid me my retainer in gold coins from South Africa.

After the preliminaries the case was assigned to trial before Judge Norbert Ehrenfreund. Ehrenfreund had been a prosecutor and later the chief trial attorney for the Public Defender's office. The prosecutor was the top arson specialist in the District Attorney's office. He was smart and wanted to win this case. In a criminal case the prosecutor is seated closest to the jury. As we were in the process of choosing a jury, I saw a large bound book on council table in view of the prospective jurors saying in bold letters, ***ARSON-INSURANCE FRAUD.*** I asked him to put it away because I though this might misrepresent to the prospective jurors

Judge Norbert Ehrenfreund

about the nature of the trial since insurance was not involved. He laughed and told me to get lost. I asked for a hearing out of the presence of the prospective jurors to take the matter of the book up. We went into chambers and I asked the prosecutor to bring his book with him. When we got into chambers I asked the Judge to look at the book and complained of the likelihood of confusing the jury. The prosecutor complained bitterly and said it was necessary in his questioning of the prospective jurors. The Judge reached a compromise position and told him to keep it covered when not in actual use.

Back to the courtroom we went. The prosecutor put a paper over the cover and we continued selecting the jury. It wasn't long before the paper was gone and the book was in full view. I didn't want to seem picky to the Judge so I leaned over and whispered to the prosecutor. I told him if the book wasn't put away I was going to John Holt's (a famous trial lawyer) office and borrow a book bigger and bolder that said, *CASES WHERE THE INNOCENT HAVE BEEN CONVICTED!* I think he believed me because his book vanished.

It was a long trial and took longer than usual because it was the first case in our county to have a blind juror serve on a panel after the Federal Handicap law went into effect. I knew I wanted this person to serve when in response to a question by the Judge he said in high school he had participated in track but gave it up because he couldn't stay in his lane.

The jury found the defendant not guilty and I was never paid the rest of my fee or heard from him again.

THE PERUVIAN DWARF

Illustration by Ray Blavatt

She was an exchange student from Peru attending San Diego State College, about 18 years old, three feet tall with red flowing hair. One of my former professors from State College asked me to help her.

She needed legal help after being struck in the intersection by an automobile while crossing University at Park Boulevard, an unusually wide crossing. Her left leg was broken and she sustained multiple cuts and abrasions over the rest of her tiny body. She told me she was crossing University Avenue on the green light on the west side headed north, when hit by the car, which was turning left from Park Boulevard. The driver didn't see her but said when he turned left, the light in his direction was yellow. The insurance company for the driver refused to discuss settlement contending the dwarf was crossing illegally which caused her to be struck by their insured. We maintained she started across when the light turned green but, because of her size and the width of the intersection, couldn't make it across while the light was green and the driver had a duty to watch for persons crossing in front before turning.

When the trial started, I brought into the courtroom an antique high chair for my client to sit in so she could see what was going on in the courtroom. The defense attorney angrily objected saying it was a ruse to gain sympathy. When I explained that my client had a right to see and couldn't from a conventional chair, the kindly, intelligent judge agreed and overruled the objection. At a recess during jury selection, the adjuster for the driver's insurance company made a fair offer and we settled the case.

The defense lawyer was sore about the high chair and didn't speak to me for several months.

THE SAILOR AND
THE BANK VICE PRESIDENT

I don't remember how he happened to come to me. He was charged with drunk driving. Johnny was a young Navy enlisted man who had been drinking downtown at one of the Navy hangouts. It was about 10 p.m. on Friday night and he was driving home when he collided with a car coming out of the parking lot at the Cotton Patch on Midway Drive. The occupants of the other car were a vice president of one of the branches of the Bank of America and his "trophy" wife. The VP was in his middle sixties, balding and overweight. His wife was in her late twenties and was a teller at the branch where her husband worked.

Johnny was seriously injured in the collision. His right leg, arm and shoulder were broken. The bank vice president and his wife had superficial injuries. When the police arrived at the scene the bank vice president raised up such a scene that the police dragged Johnny from his car and threw him into the patrol car. The scene was witnessed by a number of customers of the Cotton Patch who came outside when they heard the collision. One of the witnesses was a nurse from Ocean Beach. She was so angry at the way the police treated Johnny and the scene that the bank vice president made, she was more than willing to testify for Johnny at the trial.

It was conceded that the sailor had too much to drink. The defense was that drunk or sober he didn't cause the collision. Our traffic reconstruction expert said that the bank vice president pulled out in front of Johnny's car, thus could have avoided the collision. The jury agreed and the sailor was found not guilty.

After the criminal trial since the issue was causation I brought a suit for Johnny against the bank vice president. When I filed the suit all hell broke out. The bank vice president had retained Tom Golden to bring a civil suit for damages for himself and his wife. I had gotten the jump on Golden and he had to file a cross complaint. Now, everything got crazy. Johnny's insurance carrier hired a well-known insurance defense lawyer, Marshall Foreman, to defend Johnny on the cross complaint, and the bank vice president's insurance company hired another well-known defense lawyer, Dutch Higgs, to defend the complaint filed by Johnny.

Dutch, at the time, was a Regent of the University of California and a well-known public figure.

The case was assigned to Department 12 before Judge Robert W. Conyers, a very respected San Diego Superior Court Judge. Conyers had, some years earlier, been a partner in Dutch's law firm, but also lived in Ocean Beach, which I believed showed excellent judgment. In my mind that balanced the ledger!

This was a jury trial so the first order was to select the jury. Judge Conyers spent some time asking questions of the prospective jurors. From the Judge's questions we learned that two of the prospective jurors worked for the University of California at La Jolla. One was an older man and the other much younger. I questioned the jurors after the Judge finished. Then Dutch took over. He asked a number of questions to the twelve prospective jurors in the jury box. When he came to the older male employee of the University he said, "You will probably learn that I am a Regent of the University of California. Would you tend to favor my side just because of this?"

This juror who was obviously impressed replied, "Of course not, Mr. Higgs, I can be totally fair."

I nudged my co-counsel Marshall and said let's go to the bench. When we got to the side bar, I complained bitterly that Dutch was trying to gain favorite treatment from these two jurors. I moved for a mistrial. Dutch protested innocence and the judge denied my motion. Shortly after this question Dutch moved on. When

Dutch got to the younger University of California employee, he was not going to repeat the question because he knew this young juror knew who he was. Dutch simply asked this juror if he had heard the questions he had asked of the other jurors, and if there was any answer to any question that he would like to mention. The juror thought for a few seconds and Dutch, seeing the pause, asked if he wanted to say anything. This juror responded, "Yes" and Dutch asked him to explain. The juror then said, "I question your motives in telling us you were a Regent of the University when you knew I worked there."

Dutch's face got white and I kicked Marshall saying, "Yes". When it came time to exercise challenges I excused the older employee of the University and Dutch excused the younger one.

The next juror called to the box was a retired Navy chief. When it came my turn to ask questions I asked he if he had heard Dutch tell everyone that he was a Regent of the University of California! He allowed he had and then I said, "Chief, you understand that a Regent is appointed by the Governor and Mr. Higgs is a very important person and lawyer." The chief said he understood, and then I said, "Chief, if it comes out that I am a former lifeguard from Ocean Beach and I represent a plain enlisted sailor, will that be held against us?"

With that Dutch exploded and up to the bench we went. Dutch was fuming, and accused me of everything in the book. Judge Conyers motioned to me not to respond and told Dutch that he had started it and for both of us to behave.

During the trial the two insurance defense lawyers settled the case. The bank vice president's carrier paid the sailor and the sailor's insurance carrier paid the bank vice president and his wife.

Later when I talked to the jury most said they were going to rule for the sailor, but you never know.

GREEN RUDD

Green was a big black man in his late twenties. He looked as if he could have been a tackle on a professional football team. He was arrested when he was in the company of a friend who sold narcotics to an undercover narc officer and was charged with being an accessory to the sale of narcotics. Green told me he was just along for the ride and didn't know his friend was going to sell dope.

When the case went to trial we were assigned to Judge William Sommer. Sommer was smart, fair and he let the lawyers try their cases. Years later, when I became a judge, I learned how difficult it was not to interject myself into the case in a jury trial. After the jury was selected and opening statements had been given by the prosecutor and both defense lawyers, the co-defendant made a deal and entered a plea to a lesser offense. This plea bargain, made during a recess and away from the jury, included a promise by the co-defendant to testify against Green.

Judge William Sommer

When the co-defendant took the stand he gave damaging testimony against Green, but it did not include the exculpatory evidence he had told the prosecutor during the bargaining session. When it came my time to cross-examine him, I asked him about the plea bargain and the lessor offense he was allowed to enter in exchange for his testimony, and also if he hadn't told the prosecutor that Rudd didn't know about the dope and the sale?

He said, "Yes."

And then I asked him "Didn't the prosecutor tell you that if you didn't testify against Rudd, there would be no deal?"

He answered, "Yes."

When this happened, the Prosecutor jumped to his feet, almost screaming and objected saying:

"This is the most unethical thing I have ever heard, because it invades the attorney-client privilege."

I was stunned by this objection. After a moment I got it together and told the Judge that the Prosecutor did not represent the witness and the co-defendant's lawyer had told me what was said during the plea bargain conference. The Judge agreed and overruled the objection and the trial proceeded. Green ultimately took the stand and denied any involvement. The Prosecutor was unable to shake his story and the case went to the jury.

While the jury was deliberating, toward the end of the day I stopped by the courtroom and sat on a bench outside the front door. It had been a long day and I put my head in my hands and rested my eyes. I must have gone to sleep because Judge Sommer's bailiff woke me and told me the jury had gone home for the night.

The next day, the jury reached a verdict of not guilty. Judge Sommer thanked the jury for their service and excused them. After the jury left the court room the Judge read the riot act to Green and told him, "You are lucky because I believe you are guilty."

Green and the prosecutor left and I sat there for several moments reflecting on the result. Finally, I gathered my files and left. As I walked down the hall toward the escalators, one of the jurors stepped out from a doorway, grabbed me by the arm and said, "Mr. Baxley, when we left for the evening yesterday, I saw you seated on the bench outside the court praying for Divine Guidance and I knew a lawyer like you wouldn't be representing a guilty person, so we gave him the benefit of the doubt."

I never told Green about this. I just let him continue to believe I was a great lawyer.

PAUL LOWE

Paul Lowe

He was one of the original Chargers. He played football at Oregon State and came to the Chargers as a free agent in 1960 when they were still in Los Angeles. At that time the club was owned by Eugene Klein and Sam Shulman. In 1965 he borrowed $50,000 from Shulman and Klein to buy a liquor store at Logan and Euclid, an all black area of the city. Their lawyer, Stacy Sullivan, formed a corporation. Paul and his wife Sophie were two of the directors and Shulman was the third. As security Shulman and Klein took 51 percent of the stock as security for the note with the understanding that once it was paid the stock would be transferred to Paul and Sophie. Paul's salary at the time of the purchase of the liquor store was $25,000 a year, paid over a twelve-month period. The note was payable at $1,000 a month. In 1966, Paul was injured most of the football season and did not perform up to the expectations of the coaches and ownership. They decided to put the fear of God into Paul so they started holding back his monthly $1000 deferred compensation payments. Paul was beside himself and came to Harry Johnston who had been an assistant coach. Harry referred Paul to me and I set up a meeting with Shulman to see if the dispute could be resolved. This meeting was at a hotel in Mission Valley. Shulman kept me waiting for about an hour. When he finally got to the meeting, he immediately started accusing Paul of dogging it and of costing the Chargers the AFC championship, which was lost to Buffalo by over 30 points. About the only thing I managed to ask was, "Did you expect an offensive back to keep Buffalo from scoring all those points in the championship game?" The meeting ended with Shulman storming out.

The next thing that happened was Shulman and Klein called a meeting of the shareholders of Paul's Liquor Store. Since it looked ominous, I had Paul and Sophie sign proxies to a law partner of mine who attended the meeting at Higg's law firm. This was quite a scene. Paul and I and the lawyer from my office showed up to learn that Shulman and Klein had given their proxy to a lawyer from their lawyer's law firm. Neither Shulman nor Klein attended this meeting. The meeting started by their lawyers making a motion to elect new officers of the corporation. Since they could elect two of the three directors and take control of Paul Lowe's Liquor Store, they proceeded to elect two young lawyers from their law firm. Paul elected the other director. Paul was beside himself. He could see his business being destroyed. At that point I asked Paul to give me the keys to the store and told him to call Sophie and tell her what happened and tell her to leave the store. Paul gave me the keys and I tossed them on the table and said the store was under their control and they better get there in a hurry before it was looted! Faces turned red, then purple and a recess was taken. In about five minutes they came back, receded the previous action and again elected Paul and Sophie as President and Vice-President/Treasurer. Soon Paul was paid his deferred compensation and traded to Kansas City. It worked out pretty well for Paul: he got his store and a share of the purse for Kansas City's winning the Superbowl in 1969.

THE BLACK SATIN SHEETS

I met Bob Rodman in Nassau, in the Bahamas, in the early seventies at a birthday party. He was a tall, good-looking man in his early forties with a Hapsburg jaw. Rodman was wealthy and came from the family that owned Alliance Machine Company of Alliance, Ohio. We struck it off right away. At a party one hot night, after many rum drinks, he told me about his divorce in progress in Northern California. He felt he was losing because his wife's lawyer (from Los Angeles) had hired a local lawyer to assist in the proceedings who was a poker-playing friend of the Judge hearing the case. Rodman asked me to come to the trial and watch. After we returned to the United States I attended the hearing and Rodman was right. He got hammered! He told me he wanted to appeal and asked me to represent him. I told him I would, but I did not paint a rosy picture about the prospects of success. I recommended that before we started the appeal that it would be worth a trip to Los Angeles to see if the case could be settled. He agreed and I met with his wife's attorney in Los Angeles. At that meeting I managed to settle the case to Rodman's satisfaction. He asked me to send him a bill. I knew he had already spent nearly one hundred thousand dollars on attorney's fees, and I told him to pay my out-of-pocket expenses and we would call it square. He paid my costs and several weeks later, I received a package in the mail from him. This package contained a beautiful pair of king sized, black satin sheets and pillowcases monogrammed with my initials RCB. I was speechless. I used them once but they were so

83

slippery they weren't practical to use. Besides, they had to be dry-cleaned after each use, which was expensive.

If you are wondering what the point of this story is, hang in there. The sheets sat in the closet in a dust bag until late one August day. Every year, an invitational two-man volleyball tournament was held at the north end of La Jolla Shores beach, where the sea wall ends.

Two close friends, Mike and Patty, had been a part of every tournament from the start. At the time of the first tournament, they lived in Del Mar several miles to the north of where the tournament was held. By now Mike's job had taken him and Patty to London, England, where they now lived. He and Patty came back to San Diego each year for the tournament and this year planned to stay with me at my home in Ocean Beach. I planned to give them my bedroom with the king-size bed. In honor of my loving friends, I put the black satin sheets on the bed for their enjoyment.

They arrived late Friday afternoon from New York and immediately went to a pre-tournament party. They finally got to my house about midnight. I made a big deal about giving them my bedroom and with a flourish, threw back the covers and unveiled the black satin sheets. I told them the story of my acquisition and they were duly impressed. I made an exit and left them to get ready for sleep.

Sometime later, I crept through the dark house, cracked open their door and whispered, "No slipping and sliding," never dreaming they might be "doing it!" I heard Patty gasp then two thuds as they both slipped off the bed onto the floor. Patty said, "That son of a bitch. He probably planned this!"

I fell to the floor laughing uncontrollably until my side was splitting.

The next morning when I saw Mike, he told me that Patty was pissed and that I had better not tell anyone at the beach about the incident. I gave him my word. However, when I got to the beach that morning Patty, not trusting me, had told everyone what happened. Oh ye of so little faith!

She didn't think it was very funny at the time but now as we have all grown older we have a good laugh about the incident.

HOUSTON RIDGE

Houston Ridge

Ron Mix

Houston Ridge was born in Madra, California in 1944. He was signed by the Chargers in 1966 before he finished San Diego State College where he played linebacker and was a star on the track team. In 1966 he weighed 230 pounds and was considered one of the strongest men around.

The coaches thought he was too slow to play linebacker so he was put on a weight-gaining program so he could play defense tackle. Houston trusted the coaches and did what he was told. Soon he weighed 265 pounds and his strength gained accordingly and soon became the strongest player on the Charger's team. The way he increased his weight so dramatically was he was given steroids. At the time the Chargers employed a strength coach named Alvin Roy. Roy had been a coach for the Olympic weight lifting team and had learned about this "Miracle Drug" from the Russians. He convinced the coaches to encourage its use. The club provided the pills and went so far as to fine players who refused to take them.

The trainer put a pill in a cup at lunch and the coach ordered the players to take them. Apparently no one investigated the side effects or even cared if the drug produced the desired effects.

The use of this drug produced the desired effect in Houston. He got bigger and stronger! Many other prescription drugs were also in use by the Chargers. This included vast amounts of amphetamines, muscle relaxants, pain pills and sleeping tablets. Many of these drugs were purchased in bulk directly from the manufacturers. Others were purchased in bulk from a local pharmacy on a prescription from the team physician. The drugs purchased from the pharmacy were on prescriptions in the names of the coaches and management personnel. For example, if the trainer needed sleeping tablets the doctor would fill the prescription in the name of the head coach for 1000 Seconal. The trainer would pick them up and keep them in the training room and pass them out when players needed some. No records were maintained as to what player was getting what drug or the amount and frequency of the filling of orders.

In October, 1969, Houston was injured in a game with Miami. In those years the Chargers made an East Coast swing of three games. In this particular swing the Chargers played consecutive weeks in Miami, New York and Boston. In Miami, Houston was given an examination by the team physician, Dr. E. Paul Woodward, who thought he had bruised his hip. No x-rays were taken even though Houston was in tremendous pain. The coaches just thought he was "dogging it" and tried to make him work it out. He went those three weeks trying to practice, but his injury got worse.

Finally, after returning to San Diego, Dr. Woodward ordered a x-ray and discovered that Houston had broken his hip. As a result of the forced weight bearing and the failure to properly treat Houston, the bone in his femur started to die. This ended his football career!

Houston was referred by Ron Mix, his teammate who I met as a law student at the University of San Diego. Ron had graduated in 1965 but was still playing professional football. Ron was considered one of the great offensive tackles ever to play the game.

I filed the lawsuit in 1970 alleging negligence and medical malpractice. The named defendants were the team doctor, the team trainer, the pharmacist, the Chargers and the National Football League. The team doctor was represented by Wes McInnis, the pharmacist by John S. Rhoades, the trainer and the Chargers by Stacy Sullivan and the National Football League by Frank Rothman. The reputations of the opposing lawyers were formidable! This group consisted of some of the finest trial lawyers in America. Their first move was to ask the judge to throw out the complaint alleging, among other things, that the complaint did not state a cause of action against them. The first hearing was heard by Judge Hugo Fisher. Judge Fisher was smart, but known for taking his time in deciding cases. At the oral arguments all these high-priced lawyers showed up for the hearing. I felt overwhelmed. *Judge Hugo Fisher*

The judge took the case under submission. I had Houston come to the hearing and when we were leaving as I was walking down the hall, the lawyer for the Chargers yelled at me for having my "crippled client" in court to get sympathy from the judge. It was all I could do to keep from going after him. Sullivan had been one of my professors in law school and had given me the lowest grade I ever received even though it was the highest grade for that class.

After several weeks I called Judge Fisher's court clerk and asked her if the Judge had ruled on the motions. She said he had not. I waited another week without hearing so the next week I started showing up in the judge's courtroom every morning where he could see me. He finally got the drift of my appearances and issued his ruling overruling the defendants' legal attacks.

By then I was convinced that the legal power on the other side was going to be more than I could handle. Some months before at a legal seminar I had been introduced to a Los Angeles lawyer, David Harney. Harney was considered one of the great plaintiff's legal malpractice attorneys in America. He was in San Diego trying a case and I arranged to meet him after court one day. I was impressed with our meeting and told him about the case and asked if he was interested in associating as co-counsel. He agreed and I filed the association and served the defense attorneys. Things changed dramatically. We started taking depositions, obtaining records and suddenly the defendants' attitudes changed. This discovery showed that the trainer was ordering drugs in bulk directly from the drug manufacturer in most cases and others through the pharmacy. In the case of drugs ordered from the pharmacy the prescriptions would be given from the team doctor in the names of administrative personnel and coaches. The name of the head coach, Sid Gilman, was used for the sleeping tablets. In fairness to the coach I don't think he knew what was going on. I remember when we took his deposition I asked him if he had a sleeping problem. He was annoyed and answered he did not. I then showed him a prescription for 1000 Seconal tablets in his name paid for by the Chargers and he was genuinely surprised.

The evidence of drugs being given to Chargers players by the team doctor and trainer was staggering. The trainer was passing out diet pills in handfuls. These were used to produce rage at the levels being taken. Then came the sleeping tablets, pain pills, muscle relaxants and you name it. They had everything to keep the player in action. The drug abuse was staggering. Because of this evidence the defendants settled the case very favorable to Houston. The amount of the settlement was made public but the amounts the various defendants contributed to the total would not be divulged and no agreement was made about discussing the facts of the case. After it was announced that the case had settled I started receiving calls from reporters all over the country. I didn't give anything to anyone until the settlement check was cashed and disbursed. Then, at the suggestion of a judge I gave everything to Jack Murphy, the sports editor of the *San Diego Union*. The *San Diego Union* gave the case extensive coverage and Murphy was nominated for a Pulitzer Prize for his coverage of the story. These stories invoked such interest that Congress started an investigation and was considering passing laws regulating drug use in professional football. In the middle of this controversy the Commissioner of Professional Football agreed to pass rules regulating drug use by the teams. I have received most of the credit for this lawsuit, but it would never have happened without David Harney.

David died this year. He was a great lawyer and we remained friends until his death.

Coach Gilman's Granddaughter

Many years after the football player drug cases my friend, Ron Mix, asked me if I would help his coach with a problem. He told me Gilman's granddaughter was in trouble over a number of California Vehicle Code violations. I said I would be happy to help. We met and began trying to resolve her problems which were considerable.

I met with the deputy of the City Attorney's office and negotiated a resolution very favorable to the granddaughter. It didn't take much time so when the coach asked me for a bill I told him I took care of the matter as a favor to Ron. He was most grateful and insisted on taking me to dinner. We met at Quiggs, a nice restaurant in Ocean Beach behind the Lifeguard Station. Coach Gilman, his wife, his daughter and Ron and Patty Mix were present. We had a nice dinner and I left for home. Ron told me later, as he and the coach were leaving the restaurant, the coach put his arm around Ron and said, "You know, I love that boy!" (meaning me).

Because of the bad feelings resulting from the Houston Ridge case that was probably the best turnaround that ever happened to me as a lawyer.

TOM BASS

"...Who is the man you ask/he's known by different names/speed-diet pills-or benny/he answers/to all these /initially/he's used for "PEP"/soon/the man/assumes bigger roles/endurance, courage and performance/all seem to come from him/and there/before your eyes/you find/that you now need /to swallow/those tiny little pills/to just go and play the game.."

—Pro Football From the Inside
Tom Bass (In Pro, 1974)

He is a big, fierce looking man. He still had three years to run on his contract as a Charger defensive coordinator when the Chargers decided to hire new assistant coaches. Management replaced Bass and three other assistant coaches. They paid their salaries for the remainder of their contracts, but refused to pay other benefits such as contributions to retirement, medical-dental-life insurance, automobile allowance and tickets to the games. Three of these coaches hired me to represent them to obtain these benefits. The other one declined, afraid he would never be able to get another coaching job if he got involved.

The coaches' written contracts all had a standard NFL arbitration clause that required such disputes to be settled by the NFL Commissioner's office. An arbitration demand was made and the case was set for a hearing in San Diego. A bright, young lawyer named Al Hartunian (now a San Diego trial judge) represented the Chargers. The case took several days to present to the arbitrator and the Commissioner eventually ruled in favor of Bass and the other coaches on the major items. He did hold that the Chargers were not required to give the coaches either the automobile allowance or the tickets. The major items, contributions to retirement and health-dental-life insurance amounted to a cash equivalent of around $150,000 per coach, another thorn in the side of Chargers owner Gene Klein.

THE KIDS, THE GAME WARDEN AND THE CLAMS

*Jeff Moore, Jenny Moore, Leslie Caperton, Linda & Bret Baxley, Betsy Moore &
Susan Caperton*

About thirty miles north of San Diego the San Diego Gas & Electric Company has a large power plant on a lagoon next to the ocean. The plant uses ocean water to cool its machines. Once the cool seawater from the ocean is used, it is pumped into the lagoon and runs back to sea through a small channel. The warm seawater in the lagoon from the plant is a perfect environment for clams.

This bed of clams was discovered by Ricky Grigg, a famous marine biologist and Ricky shared the spot with me. In those days, the limit for these clams was fifty per person. Kids didn't need a fishing license.

In my lifeguard days the Fish & Game Wardens suspected I was gathering over the limit for abalone and lobster and I was often under surveillance. Although stopped and searched many times, I was always legal. This really annoyed the game wardens, especially William Mansburger.

While I was working on the Court of Appeal right after law school one Saturday, on a particularly low tide, I invited Justice Gerald Brown (my boss) to come clamming with me and my group of kids and their parents. So off we went to the power plant lagoon. To get to the spot we parked in a tomato field just to the west of the railroad tracks and climbed down to the edge of the lagoon where the clams lived under the sand. The tide was perfect and we started digging. The kids didn't get many clams but they had a great time playing in the mud. With the adults digging we gathered limits for everyone. With our loaded pails we started up the cliff toward our cars.

As we reached the top and started through the tomato plants, Mansburger jumped from behind a bush and said, "Baxley, I want to see your licenses and check your clams."

We put down the pails and Mansburger started counting, as the kids, the parents and Justice Brown watched. About a third of the way through one bucket, he recognized Justice Brown. Mansburger's face turned white. He thumbed through a few more clams and said, "I guess you're legal." He left and we picked up our clams and went on our way. Disappointed again!

Years later when I was appointed as a Superior Court Judge, I received a note from Mansburger of congratulations and wishing me well. He knew he would never have to worry about me again!

ARNOLD MANDELL

It looked like one
of the worst seasons
ever for the team.
They were ready to try
anything—anything.
So they added
a new member,
Arnold Mandell.
A psychiatrist!
This is the story
of what happened
to them and
to him during...

THE NIGHTMARE SEASON

Arnold J. Mandell, M.D.

Cover of *The Nightmare Season*

He was about five feet eight inches tall and weighed about 130 pounds ringing wet. His brain was the largest part of his body and he was one of the most remarkable persons I ever met.

Arnold J. Mandell was born in 1934. He graduated from Stanford, Magna Cum Laude and completed his medical education at Tulane, graduating Salutatorian. At thirty-five he was the youngest doctor in the United States to become the Chair of a Department of Psychiatry of a major university.

In 1972 he was asked by Harland Svare, the head coach of the San Diego Chargers, to help with motivation problems of the players. This was in the middle of the Houston Ridge case and the National Football League had just implemented a policy prohibiting teams from dispensing diet and other mind-altering drugs to players as performance facilitators.

When Jack Murphy, the sports editor of the *San Diego Union* wrote a series of articles based upon depositions taken in the Ridge case, the nation was shocked. The United States Congress started an investigation, and Pete Roselle, Commissioner of Professional Football, agreed to pass rules regulating this drug abuse. This got Congress off his back but it had little effect on their continued use because players went to private sources to obtain them.

Mandell quickly learned many of the older players had become dependent on these drugs and were buying them on the street. He considered these street drugs very dangerous because of their impurities. When one ten-year veteran showed up with a handful of "Black Beauties" Mandell cornered Svare and it was decided Mandell would write individual prescriptions to these veterans who believed they could not play without them. A group of twelve players received such prescriptions from Dr. Mandell, which were filled at various pharmacies and paid for by the Chargers.

Mandell's prescriptions would have gone unnoticed had he not written an article in *Psychology Today* about the use of drugs in professional football. This article in the scientific journal was bad enough for pro-football's image but it also mentioned that Mandell was writing a book about his experiences with the Chargers.

When the owner, Eugene Klein, heard this he became incensed and sent Svare with a message to Mandell. The message was, "If  you publish that book I will make sure the University fires you and that you lose your license to practice medicine."

That was just the challenge Mandell needed. The original title of Mandell's book was *Romance of a Losing Season.* This title was scrapped by the publisher and in May 1976, Random House printed, published and distributed *The Nightmare Season.* A prepublication review was written by Jack Murphy who called *The Nightmare Season* "one of the best and truest books ever written about pro football." Klein went ballistic! He gave a scathing interview which was printed in the *San Diego Union* accusing Mandell of writing thousands of prescriptions of amphetamines to Chargers' players.

Arnold J. Mandell

His threat became a reality when the California Board of Medical Quality Assurance filed an accusation against Mandell charging him with prescribing dangerous drugs without a medical indication, gross negligence and gross incompetence.

To establish his defense he needed the proof I had obtained in the Ridge case. Other lawyers he consulted told him he should hire me because of my work and drug records I had obtained in the Ridge case.

I met with Arnold and agreed to represent him. Thus began one of the most incredible journeys of my legal life.

The California Attorney General's office was in charge of the prosecution and they assigned a top-flight deputy, Alvin J. Korobkin, to handle the case. Al was a bright, handsome young man who was an able advocate. Korobkin did his undergraduate at Occidental and attended UCLA Law School where he served on the Law Review. After his graduation in 1965 he started working for the Attorney General's office.

An Administrative Law Judge was assigned to hear the case. She was very bright. The hearings went on for weeks. We started in a small hearing room in the State Building. It was very crowded and I suggested to the Judge to see if there was a courtroom available for use in the County Court House a block away. The Presiding Judge of the Municipal Court gave permission to use a vacant court on the second floor. We moved to these more spacious quarters and conducted the hearings. During the proceedings two psychiatrists who were drug experts and Klein and Svare testified for the AG. Both of the drug experts were there because they had their own troubles with the Board of Medical Quality Assurance and were hoping to help their own cases. Klein was there reeking with venom and out to make good his threat to ruin Mandell.

One of the Attorney General's experts who testified against Mandell was impeached by a Superior Court Judge who said this doctor's reputation for competence and character for truthfulness was bad. I asked the Judge if he knew the AG's doctor and he said he did and the circumstances of this knowledge. The Judge said he had testified many times in his court on the Mental Health calendar. Based on his contacts with the doctor he was asked if he knew his reputation for being a competent drug expert and his character for truthfulness. He allowed he did and was then asked if his character for those traits was good or bad? The Judge said bad and that ended the direct examination.

Korobkin could not resist cross-examining the Judge. He started asking specifics and the Judge gave a very damaging account of the acts that led to his opinions. After about a half-hour, Al saw he was digging a deep hole and quick. I took the Judge on redirect examination and went into the damaging details of the facts he relied upon to reach his opinions. This ended the testimony for the day and we recessed for the day.

The next morning the Deputy made a motion to strike his cross-examination and my redirect. He told the Judge he had made a mistake and wanted to correct his error. I didn't think it was necessary to reply, but the Judge wanted to hear my position. I told her just because he didn't like the answers that was no reason to strike the testimony. To my shock the Judge granted his motion and struck his cross and my redirect examination of the Judge. I had a sinking feeling that we were going to lose no matter what the evidence showed.

Svare testified. It was obvious he liked Mandell and didn't want to hurt him, but he was afraid of Klein. At one point in Svare's cross-examination he went off on a tangent about players using pot, and I interrupted asking if it wasn't true that he was so concerned with players using pot he wasn't listening when Mandell was telling him about the amphetamines. He remembered this but said he was more worried with pot because it made the players want to make love instead of war.

Mandell had lined up some of the world's leading psycho-pharmacologists to testify for him. I had prepared written hypothetical questions relating to each player. These were given to Korobkin in advance and I told him how I was going to use them. When I called my first expert witness, I handed him the first written hypothetical question and asked him if he had read it. He said he had. I asked him to assume the facts were true and if he had an opinion of whether Mandell had been guilty of clearly excessive prescribing. Korobkin objected as an improper hypothetical. To my amazement the objection was sustained. I had previously marked each written hypothetical question to each player as an exhibit and I told the judge this was done to expedite the hearing. The Judge was not moved and I was required to read each question to the expert. About half way through the first question she got the point, and I was allowed to give the experts the various hypotheticals and was permitted to ask if they had read them and to assume the facts stated were true and their opinions. This procedure saved hundreds of hours.

The evidence finally concluded and the Judge took the matter under submission. Several weeks later we received her written decision in which she found Dr. Mandell guilty of prescribing dangerous drugs without a medical indication (Business and Professions Code, Section 2399.4), but not guilty of gross negligence or gross incompetence (Business and Professions Code Sections 2361 (b) and 2361(c).

When I called Dr. Mandell with the news he was upset and didn't want to go any further with the case. I explained the review procedure and implored him to continue. He finally agreed and a Writ of Mandamus was filed in the Superior Court for a review of the decision. The case was assigned to Judge Wesley Buttermore. Buttermore was a fair judge and an excellent scholar. Mandell was lucky; we could not have had a better assignment! In this proceeding the Judge has a new trial on the record of the administrative hearing. Each side filed briefs. The case was argued and the Judge took it under submission. During the administrative proceeding a series of Doonesbury cartoons were published nation-

Judge Wesley B. Buttermore

ally based on the case. One was very much on point and I included in my brief.

To the utter dismay of Eugene Klein, Judge Buttermore ruled in Mandell's favor and dismissed the case. In those days if one side requested it the prevailing party was required to prepare and submit finding of facts and conclusions of law supporting the decision. The other side then could object and submit other findings and conclusions. In my proposed findings I included a number of findings that would have allowed the Judge to award attorneys' fees, if the Judge found the action was filed in bad faith.

I never expected the Judge to grant attorneys' fees, but I

wanted to tweak the AG's office. I was not awarded those fees but I received a totally unexpected benefit. One of the first findings eulogized Mandell as, "Dr. Mandell's professional reputation as a research scientist and clinician, and his reputation for the character traits of truth, honesty and veracity was and are of the highest order. Dr. Mandell is one of a limited number of scientists in the relatively new field of psychopharmacology which he has practiced for 17 years."

Korobkin did file objections to the findings, but was so intent about the bad faith findings, he only objected to those directed at attorneys' fees. During argument Judge Buttermore asked if there were the only findings he objected to and Al said, "Yes." The Judge ruled in his favor on the attorneys' fee findings but the rest stood.

After the findings were signed and became official, Mandell had hundreds of copies made and mailed them to the scientific world.

The *Nightmare Season* didn't turn out to be a best seller and it resulted in a libel suit against Mandell by one of the players named in the book.

KLEIN V. AL DAVIS & THE RAIDERS

Al Davis

My personal introduction to Al Davis was in a medical malpractice suit I filed for Mike Siani against the Raiders and its team physician. Mike had his big toe dislocated and the team doctor failed to diagnose the injury. In succeeding weeks he was given injections and forced to practice and play which caused the joint to develop necrosis. This ended his playing career. In the Siani case I took the deposition of Davis. The Siani suit was settled before trial, but apparently Davis had remembered the deposition.

Much later Eugene Klein (principal owner of the San Diego

Chargers Football Club) filed a malicious prosecution action against Davis and the Raiders in San Diego. This suit arose out of Klein's being named as a defendant by the Raiders in the antitrust suit filed in Los Angeles against Klein, Roselle, the owner of the Los Angeles Rams, and the National Football League over the proposed move of the Raiders to Los Angeles. During the course of that action the Federal Judge, to simplify it, dismissed the action against Klein and the other individual defendants.

The Raiders and Davis won the antitrust action. The lawyers for the Raiders were Joseph L. Alioto and Moses Lasky, two famous California lawyers from San Francisco. Alioto was the former Mayor of San Francisco and was, at that time, married to the daughter of the owner of the Boston Patriots. Because of the family connection the Patriots were the only NFL team not named as a defendant in the antitrust suit. Lasky was a great scholar, legal writer and an exceptional trial lawyer. Lasky's name was frequently mentioned as a candidate for an appointment to the California Supreme Court.

Klein hated Davis and the Raiders because the Raiders consistently beat the Chargers and Al was not a person who could be intimidated by Klein. Right after testifying during the Raiders' antitrust lawsuit Klein suffered a heart attack. He blamed Al for causing the heart attack and filed suit in the San Diego Superior Court because Al and the Raiders made him a party to the antitrust action.

Klein hired a clever, flamboyant San Francisco trial lawyer Joe Cotchett to represent him. Cotchett, who had an enormous ego, had represented the Rams in the antitrust suit and didn't like either Davis or Alioto.

Alioto told Davis the lawsuit wasn't any good and he would have it thrown out of court. A motion was brought by Alioto's office to have the complaint dismissed because the complaint did not state a cause of action. This motion was denied and the case

proceeded toward a trial. Realizing that it might go to trial in San Diego, Alioto recommended that Davis hire a local lawyer. While searching, Al asked Ron Mix for a recommendation and Mix gave him my name with several others. Al remembered me from the Siani case and sent a young, bright Raiders house counsel, Jeff Birren, to interview me for the job. I passed muster and was hired. One of the first things I did was to inquire if the Raiders had liability

Mike Siani

insurance that might provide a defense and cover any judgment that might be obtained by Klein. Jeff sent me the copies of the Raiders' liability polices and they specifically provided coverage for a malicious prosecution action. I told Jeff that the carrier should immediately be put on notice. Jeff told me he took up the suggestion with Al who didn't want to get his insurance involved because he still believed the suit would be thrown out of court. I then forcefully advised Al to make a demand on his insurance carrier. Alioto backed me up on this and a demand was made on the carrier to defend and indemnify the Raiders in the Klein action.

The carrier had no choice but to comply and, at my suggestion, hired a well-known and well-liked San Diego insurance defense lawyer, Gary Bailey, to work on the case with me. Before the case was scheduled to go to trial Lasky prepared a motion for judgment on the pleadings and this was set for a hearing before Judge Mack Lovett. The motion was argued and the Judge took it under submission. A week or so later we received a ruling denying the motion. Years later, and after I had become a judge, Mack told me that he was considering granting the motion but he talked to another judge whose opinion he valued, and that judge told him that he should deny the motion and "let Klein and Davis fight it out." As it eventually turned out Judge Lovett was right, but it would have spoiled the good show that followed.

A settlement conference before trial was set before Judge Ted Todd. Usually it is necessary for the Plaintiff to appear in person with his lawyer at the conference. If the Defendant is covered by liability insurance the Defense lawyer who will handle the trial and the adjuster for the insurance carrier with authority must be present at the conference. In this case Judge Todd ordered both Klein and Davis to appear in person. When I told Davis that the Judge had ordered him to be present he was mad. He still believed the case was no good and motivated by spite. He came but was very unhappy. I suspected, and in retrospect believe, Todd just wanted to meet the two combatants.

Even though the Raiders' carrier offered a lot of money just to avoid substantial attorneys' fees and costs of defense Klein's demands were so large the case didn't come close to settling.

Finally, the day to start the trial arrived and the case was assigned to Judge Gilbert Harelson. This was to be Harelson's last case before he retired. I learned later, Harelson had asked the Presiding Judge to send him the case.

Harelson had been a paratrooper in World War II and was very bright, with a caustic tongue often at the expense of the person subject of his wit. I learned much later that Davis had found out that Harelson had even been a guest of the Chargers and sat in the owner's box. If this had been known at the time, Harelson would never have been the trial judge.

On the first day of trial as we walked down the hall toward the entrance to Harelson's department I saw a large group of persons wearing Raider jackets led by Marcus Allen's father. I should have seen that this set the stage for a trial not about malicious prosecution but another battle between the Raiders against the Chargers.

When the trial started, in a chamber conference, Cotchett suggested to Harelson that he wear a referee's shirt, have a whistle under his robe and a yellow flag. After some legal arguments Cotchett suggested he pull off his robe, blow his whistle and drop the yellow flag. Harelson seemed to like the idea but said he wouldn't do it

Judge Gilbert Harelson

unless everyone agreed. I couldn't believe he would even consider such a thing and told Harelson we would not agree to such a stunt.

Before the jury was called I made a motion for judgment on the grounds that since the Raiders had won the antitrust suit there was probable cause to have named Klein (the general partner) in that suit. This motion was denied, but at every opportunity I renewed this motion on this ground.

The trial started and the jury was pro-Chargers. I had worn a grey tweed jacket with leather elbow patches through the trial. At one point I was alone in the courtroom when Klein walked in. He looked at me and said, "Baxley, is that the only jacket you own?"

I replied, "Yes. Does anyone need more than one coat?"

Klein just looked at me, shrugged his shoulders and walked away.

In a trial where punitive damages are sought, the rules require that the liability case be tried first. If the jury finds liability, malice and awards damages, then the same jury tries the question of punitive damages and the amount of such damages.

In the liability trial the jury found for Klein and awarded five million dollars for general damage. In his closing argument Cotchett did not argue for a specific amount suggesting it was the moral principle involved. During jury deliberations the Foreman sent the Judge a note with a question. About 10 a.m. we received a call to come to court because the jury had sent the Judge a question. I met Gary Bailey in court and Frank Pitre, a young lawyer in the Cotchett firm who had tried a good portion of the plaintiff's case was there for Klein. To our horror the note asked if the jury could award more damages than the plaintiff argued. This request was discussed and it was agreed that the Judge would tell the jury that they could award such damages as proved by the evidence. This answer was written and given to the jury just before the noon recess. We later learned that when Klein heard the question he called Roger Hedgcock, a talk show host on a local radio station, and went on the air. The conversation between Klein and Hedgcock went something like this.

Hedgcock: "I have Gene Klein, owner of the Chargers on the line who tells me the jury in his case against Al Davis and the Raiders is about ready to award him a large verdict. Is that right Gene?"

Klein: "Yes, that's right, Roger. And I want to tell everyone in San Diego that any money this jury gives me will go right to charity in this town."

Hedgcock: "So that's the message you want this jury to get?"

Klein: "Absolutely!"

This radio conversation occurred right at the time the jury left for lunch and we learned later was heard by several jurors. That same afternoon the jury returned a verdict for five million dollars. When Davis heard the verdict he was very unhappy.

The Judge set a date for the punitive damage phase. Davis called a meeting at the Raiders' headquarters to discuss this part of the trial. Present were Davis, Joe Alioto, Jeff Birren, Gary Bailey and me. When the meeting started it was clear that Davis had decided that Alioto was going to handle the punitive damage trial. Al asked Joe to summarize how he intended to try this part of the case. Joe gave about a 15-minute presentation, and when he finished, Al, who was sitting next to me, looked at me and asked what I thought about Joe's presentation. I told him I thought it was fine but I didn't think Joe was the one to do it because he had been a witness in the liability-damage phase of the trial.

Al got in my face and asked me how I would do it.

I was sore at Al so I told him that I would tell the jury that when they were asked at the start of the trial if they would give Davis and the Raiders a fair trial they lied. And when they were asked if they would listen to the Raider's evidence they lied again. "Now don't fuck it up anymore!"

Joe and Gary said no, no! But Al grabbed me by the arm and said, "Wait a minute. I like that idea."

Needless to say we didn't do it my way.

Joe tried this phase of the trial and the jury awarded another five million dollars.

After the jury returned its verdict they hung around the courtroom. I was wondering why they were hanging around when Judge Harelson came out and took the bench wearing a referee's shirt, with a whistle and carrying a yellow flag. He blew the whistle and dropped a yellow flag. I suspect, without our knowledge, Klein's lawyers provided the judge these props.

After leaving the courtroom while walking toward the exit, Joe Alioto put his arm around my shoulder and said, "Bax, I have just proved you are as good a lawyer as I am."

I loved Joe for saying that.

After the second hit we made a motion for judgment notwithstanding the verdict and new trial. Judge Harelson denied the request for judgment but granted a new trial unless Klein accepted a reduction of three million dollars on the damage verdict and three million on the punitive damage verdict. Klein was willing to accept the reduction but Davis intended to appeal.

We had another meeting in the Raiders' offices. During this meeting Cotchett called and Al told Alioto to talk to him. Cotchett was trying to get the Raiders to settle by saying that if we agreed they would go after the Raiders' insurance company. The kicker was, if Klein was unable to collect from the Raiders' insurance, then the Raiders would have to pay the judgment. I argued against this. Al handed Joe a note saying, **"Make Baxley the fall guy. He doesn't want to."**

Joe put the blame on me and the case was not settled.

The Raiders' insurance company hired Ed Lascher of Ventura to handle the appeal. The Court of Appeal reversed and entered judgment for the Raiders. After this decision I received a telephone call from Al thanking me for my work. That is the last time I spoke to Al.

Klein, Alioto, Bailey and Lascher have died. Moses Lasky is 94 years old and as far as I know is still practicing law in San Francisco. It was an exciting time in my legal life and I will never forget the kindness that Joe Alioto showed me during these events.

THE SOCIETY ISLANDS

I fancy the South Seas have claimed the pair of us.
—Faery Lands of the South Seas-Nordhoff & Hall

In the summer of 1969, I had just finished a long criminal trial and needed a rest. Over the years I had collected and read all of Charles Bernard Nordhoff and James Norman Hall books on the South Sea Islands. They wrote about life and adventure in the French Polynesia in the twenties and thirties. French Polynesia includes the Austral, Society, Gambier, Tuamotu and Marquesas Islands. My son had just turned eight and had already learned to dive. I knew some surfers from Newport Beach who had migrated to the South Seas, gone native and built some hotels they called "The Bali Hai." My son and I loaded our diving gear and boarded UTA in Los Angeles at 11 p.m. one Thursday and headed for Tahiti. We were way in the rear of the plane and slept for most of the long flight. With the time changes, we landed in Papeete on Tahiti about five in the morning. When we left the plane we walked toward the open-air baggage area and ran into Neil & Judith Morgan, friends from San Diego. They were with a group which included Walter and Betty Cronkite and their son Chip, Bob Considine and his wife Millie, Willis and Doris Player, Art and Barkle Buckwald and James Michener. You never know whom

you might run into! Neil asked what we were up to and I told him we were going diving for shells. I was too embarrassed to ask what they were doing, but I guessed a story would come from their trip. We didn't see them again. My son was too young to appreciate who he had just met.

Walter Cronkite & Neil Morgan

We spent the night in Papeete, then headed with our diving gear on the local plane to Moorea and checked into the Bali Hai.

We told the person in charge of diving that we intended to dive in the lagoon. He told us not to go because a white shark had been seen inside the lagoon. I told him that didn't bother us. He seemed troubled by my comment, and asked why? When I told him "professional courtesy," he looked puzzled. He didn't know I was a lawyer and I'm not sure he would have got it anyway. Well, we went anyway, had several great dives and collected many shells. In addition to diving we went to the top of the mountain and looked at the magnificent view toward Tahiti.

Our next stop was Raiatea, where we checked into another Bali Hai. This was the most unspoiled of the islands we visited. This hotel had a diving master named Roger. We asked Roger to take us, but he seemed very suspicious of our ability. It was here a gift got us into the best diving on the trip. I had brought an underwater camera and a new exposure meter. Roger admired it and I gave it to him. I didn't know how to use it anyway. From then on Roger took us to the best spots where we collected some rare shells.

Our next stop was Bora Bora, the most beautiful of the Islands we visited and the model island for Mitchner's Bali Hai. We stayed at the Hotel Bora Bora, in a room built on stilts over an encircling lagoon. Every morning we could smell the fresh bread baking as we arose on the placid waters surrounding us. I fully expected to run into "Bloody Mary," the leading character in the musical "South Pacific." Each day we would hike to the edge of a long curved bay to the north of the hotel, then drift with the current back to our bungalow. As we drifted, I dove for shells and collected all I wanted. I stored the live shells in some watertight bags brought from home, planning to clean them when I got home. We left our island paradise refreshed and restored. When we landed in San Diego, the baggage handler gave me a funny look because the bag of shells was really ripe. I often dream of a return to paradise!

A BIT OF LUCK
(THE RED SAILS FIRE)

The Red Sails is a well-known restaurant on the east side of the entrance to Shelter Island. A diving friend of mine, Chuck Adams, worked there in the fifties as a bartender. By the time I had finished law school and started to practice in downtown San Diego, Chuck had bought The Red Sails. We stayed close over the years. Chuck had very definite opinions about most things. You might even say he was inflexible. I had helped him with some domestic problems but had never done any work for his business.

I don't remember how I learned it, maybe through the newspaper, but the Red Sails had a major fire one evening. I went to see Chuck after the disaster. He told me that a fat fryer in the kitchen had overheated and exploded after the restaurant had closed, because a faulty thermostat had not turned off. He told me he had saved the part because of his fire insurance.

I told Chuck, "Let's have someone examine it." Chuck said, "No, it's a waste of time." I said, "Give me the fucking thermostat!"

He gave me the damaged part. Enter Dr. Wolter, Professor at San Diego State College. I had watched Dr. Wolter testify in several trials and thought he was an outstanding forensic witness. He had doctorates in medicine, physics and chemistry to mention a few. Short, chubby, with a wild head of hair, he talked with a German accent and could have been cast as a mad professor in a Disney movie. Wolter took the part to his laboratory and determined that the thermostat was defectively designed. Based on his conclusion, I filed a product liability case against General Electric, the manufacturer of the fat fryer and thermostat. General Electric hired a well-known defense law firm and Charles W. Rees to defend the action. Rees filed a cross-complaint against the manufacturer of the thermostat and Harrison Hollywood was retained to represent that manufacturer.

The first thing Rees did was to demand that I turn over the alleged defective part so that he could send it to the laboratory at GE to be examined. I told Rees that I would not give him the part without a written stipulation and order for non-destructive testing and that the part, together with the report, would be returned within sixty days. I remember I prepared the stipulation and order to have it signed by a Judge for non-destructive testing to be returned with the report. Rees thinks that happened by a written motion. In any event an order was signed by the Judge and I turned the fat fryer and thermostat over to Charlie.

Rees told me he personally delivered the parts to GE with specific instruction about the handling of the parts. Apparently, GE gave the parts to an expert for evaluation. About three months later, the part and report had not been returned. I called Rees, reminded him of the court order and told him I wanted the part and GE's report. He said he would call and find out about the delay. About two weeks later Rees called me to tell me he had the part. I told him I would stop by and pick it up. When I got to his office he handed me a box from GE. I asked him to open it so we could inspect it together. When he opened the box it contained the old fat fryer but instead of the old thermostat there was a new part. I asked him, "Where's the one I gave you?" He said, "I'll check." The next day he told me, "They have lost it."

I told Rees I was going to make a motion to strike GE's answer. This was done and GE's answer was stricken as well as their cross-complaint against Hollywood's client.

Rees suggested a settlement conference. The case settled for the full amount of the loss. I made a nice fee and Chuck Adams thought I was a hero. I didn't tell him for some years that we won because of GE's screw-up. Even with this knowledge he still thinks I am a hero. Chuck sold the Red Sails and moved to Mulege, Baja California Sur where he lives with his dog. I see him whenever I am in Mulege looking for shells.

THE RESCUE

Pearl Diver

Your friend is the man who knows all about you and still likes you.

—Elbert Hubbard

In the late fifties, Jon Lindbergh (son of aviator Charles A. Lindbergh) and I were hired by the Co-operativa in Hermosillo, Mexico, to do a diving survey of the lobster population in the middle of the Sea of Cortes. We loaded my skiff and headed southeast from San Diego to Kino Bay which is west from Hermosillo. We spent two weeks diving around the islands in the center of the Gulf of Mexico. While John was looking for lobster, I was looking for the "pearl diver" pictured in Randolph Leigh's book *Forgotten Waters*. We found lobster, but not of such quantity to make it commercially feasible to trap them. We made a fatal mistake about our conclusion that we gave the Co-op upon our return to Kino Bay. On our last day on the water we hit a spot where we found a large cave full of lobsters. We loaded the skiff. When we hit the beach and told our Mexican sponsor we didn't think there were enough lobster to make a commercial operation profitable, they didn't believe us. They started fishing and learned, at great expense, that we were right.

I had also traveled extensively in Baja on both the ocean and gulf sides. So I decided in early 1981 to get a small boat and sail from the northern end of the gulf on the Baja side to Cabo San Lucas. I started looking for a suitable craft and finally settled on a New England Surf-Sail Dory. I contracted with the Lowell's Boat Shop in Amesbury, Massachusetts to build the boat for the trip. Lowell's Boat Shop had been established in the late 1700's and was still in it original location. Pretty romantic! Well the dory was built and I took delivery in Amesbury in the late summer 1982. I drove across country in my VW van and had a trailer built in Amesbury and drove back to San Diego with the dory which I named "Spirit" in honor of Charles Lindbergh's airplane.

After returning to San Diego I spent the fall and winter planning and dreaming of my adventure. Finally, the day to leave San Diego came. I thought about starting on April 1, 1983, but some of my friends advised against this date because of the symbolism. As it turned out the first would have been perfect.

With my friends, Bob & Joan Conyers, Charlie & Nancy Faust

and Jon Lippitt, we headed with the Spirit to El Golfo which is at the north end of the Sea of Cortes on the mainland side of Mexico. Lippitt was going to bring my truck and the trailer back to San Diego and when I finished the trip in Cabo San Lucas bring me home. The journey was well known to a number of my friends who never expected to see me again.

On the morning of April 5, 1983 about 8 a.m. the adventure began. It was a beautiful day. Very little wind, the tide was low and still going out. The Spirit was launched and off I went leaving my friends waving on the beach behind as I headed south toward San Felipe by way of Consag Rock which was several miles north of San Felipe in the center of the gulf. About noon the wind freshened and I started to sail at about 5 knots. I hadn't taken into consideration the tidal change. In the upper gulf there is a very large tide change. Now the tide was coming in at about 5 knots so I wasn't going anywhere. By nightfall I was still in the upper middle of the gulf not near Consag Rock. The wind died and the moon and stars came out. I ate a cold dinner and lashed the helm of the dory to port and went to sleep. I am not sure when I woke, but the wind was blowing and the sail was flapping. I decided to lower it which required going to the bow. On the way a wave hit and I went to one side causing the Spirit to flip on its side. Now I was in the water with my boat on its side full of water and my goods floating away with the tide.

I got into the water and pulled the boat upright. It was full of water and I started bailing from outside. Finally I got enough out that I could get in and then I started bailing from the inside. I finally got most of the water out but the sail was still up. Again I went toward the bow to let it down and again the boat tipped on its side. This time the heavy tiller came loose and started to float away. I swam after it and managed to get it back to the Spirit and tied it off. This time while still in the water I lowered the sail. I righted the dory again and again bailed the water out. In the two times it overturned I lost a lot of gear. It was dark, the tide was moving rapidly so I forgot about it. I didn't feel the cold during the excitement but now I really got cold. It seemed like dawn would never arrive. I remember during the night seeing the lights of some shrimp boats to the southwest along the shore and lights from autos headed south on the road to San Felipe. By the time dawn came I was freezing and several miles off shore headed south with the outgoing tide. I rowed toward shore and beached the dory. I was unable to attach the rudder so I pulled the Spirit high on the sand and surveyed the damage. Except for one broken oar the boat was intact. I had lost my sleeping bag, clothes and a lot of gear, but fortunately a waterproof box with my money, identification and passport was safe.

I could see the highway to San Felipe in the distance and started off with some water, my money and identification to hitch a ride into town to get help. I left my log which had a list of persons to call in the event of an emergency. It was further to the highway than I had guessed. It took about three hours to reach the road through mud and quicksand. By the time I got to the highway I was covered with mud and exhausted. I finally hitched a ride with an American family into San Felipe. I was so dirty they had me ride in the back of their truck. It was about 2 p.m. when I arrived at the town. The wind was still blowing hard. I went to the beach and washed in the gulf then started looking for a panga to hire to go look for the Spirit. I finally found one and the owner and I started off to get the Spirit. The wind was blowing about 40 mph straight at us as we headed north up the gulf. When we reached the spot where I though it was we couldn't locate it. By now it was late afternoon and we were running low on gas so we headed back to town. When we got there we were running on fumes. I paid my boat operator and headed for a motel to get a room and take a shower. On the way I bought a pair of Levis and a T-shirt. When I got to the motel, because I was still covered with grime, the owner wasn't going to rent me a room until I flashed my bankroll. I went to my room, took a shower, changed clothes and headed into town to get some dinner. I spent the night at the motel and got up early the next day and headed back to the beach to rent another panga to continue the search. The weather was perfect. I had a major problem though because all the boats were hired for the day for fishing. I learned that I couldn't get a boat until late in the afternoon when the boats returned from fishing. Faced with this I made a decision to return to San Diego on the bus and get my skiff and go look for the Spirit myself. There were two buses leaving that morning. The first to Tijuana and one about an hour later to Mexicali where I could transfer to a Greyhound to San Diego. I decided to take the first bus and come back to San Diego via Tijuana. So off I went. Unknown to me the Spirit washed up at an American settlement about 5 miles north of San Felipe. The plot now thickens. A man named "Dub Cooper" (no relation to the infamous Cooper robber that parachuted from the jet with the bank loot) found the log and called Charlie Faust who started a rescue mission. As I was headed back to San Diego on the bus three small planes loaded with a rescue crew were headed south toward the Sea of Cortes. The members of the rescue team were: Mike Neil (lawyer and Marine General), Charles R. Faust (San Diego Zoo/Wild Animal Park designer, artist and friend), Jon Lippitt (who had gone with me to launch the Spirit), Neil Baxley (lawyer and my brother), John S. Rhoades (lawyer now Federal Judge), John Butler (lawyer, former San Diego Mayor and pilot of one plane), Gordon Churchill (lawyer and pilot of one plane), Dan White (lawyer) and Jim Dalby (instructor of local flying service and close friend of Charlie Faust). The rescuers circled around the upper gulf looking for me suspecting I had drowned. Dalby even landed on the beach near Coopers house to talk to Dub and look at the Spirit.

I got back to San Diego about 4 p.m. I had ridden the Trolley from TJ and got off at the stop a block from my office on 10th Avenue. When I walked in the door the secretary looked as if she had seen a ghost. My office had become the command center for the rescue operation. There was no way to notify the rescuers that I was safe at home. I was very tired by now so I got a ride home and went to bed. Meanwhile back at San Felipe, the planes had landed and they were holding a wake for me! John Butler's wife had learned that I was safe at home. John called home to tell her they were spending the night and would resume the search in the morning. When she told him I was safe at home the wake turned into a Bax-bashing ball.

The rescuers flew back the next day. I was touched by their concern but I have never heard the end of it. Faust even designed a T-shirt, the Baxley Search & Rescue Team Society was formed and several parties were held to celebrate the event. As I look back on my life this was a memorable occasion and I am touched that such wonderful people made the effort. I still think my brother felt cheated that I hadn't drowned and they had to cancel the wake!

Later I completed the voyage but in a more stable sailboat.

CONCLUSION

There was the Door to which I found no Key:
There was a Veil past which I could not see:
Some little Talk awhile of Me and Thee
There seem'd–and then no more of Thee and Me.
　　　　　　　　　　　　　　　　　—The Rubaiyat

Before I was a lawyer I was a lifeguard. As a lifeguard it was a free wheeling time that got very serious when someone's life was at risk. As a lawyer I had a lot of fun but when it counted it got very serious.

This work deals with the humorous aspects of my practice of law. I felt it was important even in the most serious cases to have some laughter as long as the jury was laughing with you, not at you!

I had the privilege of representing some very interesting people. I have not written about many because my work for them is confidential or their representation didn't fit the purpose of this remembrance; for example, the actor Lon Chaney and singer Frankie Lane. Both Lon and Frankie were wonderful persons and I was honored to do some legal work for them.

After the practice of law I was fortunate to be appointed as a Superior Court Judge by Governor Pete Wilson. In the fifth year of this duty I had a stroke which forced my retirement. I look back fondly at those wonderful years in law and the memories of a life of rescuing some poor bastard in legal trouble.

As I leave the law, I am unsettled by the change in lawyering. For too many the acquisition of wealth has become more important than saving someone caught in a legal riptide. I am grateful that I practiced at a time where law was a profession instead of a job.

As my life draws to a close I now understand the significance of the Island Princess Tithuti's last farewell to Fredrick O'Brien when she said: " We come, we do not know whence, and we go we do not know where. Only the sea endures, and it does not remember." *(White Shadows of the South Seas, p. 446)*

San Diego, California, August 20, 1999, on the day of my 70th birthday.

BIOGRAPHY

"With our eyes fixed firmly in the future,
we march confidently into the past."

—*Anonymous*

*D*uring my practice of law in San Diego I worked with and was opposed by many fine lawyers and appeared before many fine San Diego judges. These are some of these lawyers, judges and clients who are mentioned in these stories.

I have mostly said nice things about them hoping they will buy this work to share with their families and numerous friends.

JOSEPH L. ALIOTO

Born in San Francisco in 1916, he died in San Francisco in 1998. Joe obtained his law degree from Catholic University in Washington, D.C. in 1940 and for five years worked for the Antitrust Division of the United States Justice Department. In 1945 he started practicing Antitrust Law in San Francisco. He was elected Mayor of San Francisco two consecutive terms from 1968 to 1976. Joe successfully represented Al Davis and the Raiders in an antitrust suit concerning the Raiders' move to Los Angeles. Joe was one of the most charming persons I ever met and was a loyal friend.

TOM BASS

Lives in La Costa, California with his wife Michele and has three grown children. He has authored and published several books and other works on Professional Football and Poetry. He has coached and held several administrative positions on several National Football Clubs.

ALLEN BROWN

After twenty-four years with the San Diego Police Department he retired in 1974. He was a dedicated, heroic police officer and fine public servant.

GERALD BROWN

Was born in South Dakota in 1915. He was valedictorian of his high school class and lettered in football, basketball and track. He received his undergraduate degree from the University of Southern California in 1937 where he was Phi Beta Kappa. He next attended Oxford as a Rhode Scholar, and then graduated from Yale Law School in 1941. After serving in the United States Army in World War II, he went to work for the Santa Fe Railway Company on its legal staff. Later he was a partner in the Riverside law firm of Best, Best & Krieger until he was appointed as a Justice on the California Court of Appeal by Governor Pat Brown in 1963. He became Presiding Justice of the Fourth District Court of Appeal in 1965 where he served until November 1985. During his time on the bench he served on the California Judicial Council. Judge Brown received an Honorary Doctorate of Law Degree from the University of San Diego in 1973. Justice Brown was adored by his many research attorneys who gathered to honor him after his retirement. He is married to Olive and they have three grown children.

ROBERT W. CONYERS

Born in North Dakota in 1917 he was appointed to the San Diego Superior Court in 1959 and retired in 1979 after a distinguished career as a trial judge. Rated by the San Diego County Bar Association as its most intelligent and respected Judge, he currently lives in Alpine and writes extensively. Among his many accomplishments he received an Honorary Doctor of Law Degree from the University of San Diego Law School and is he is a member of the prestigious Sunset Cliffs Literary, Poetry and Philosophy Society.

AL DAVIS

Principal-Owner and Managing General Partner of the Oakland Raiders

Born on the Fourth of July, 1929 in Massachusetts he is one of the most controversial, feared and respected owners in professional football. Enshrined in the Professional Football Hall of Fame he has served as an assistant coach, head coach, commissioner of the American Football League and owner of one of the most respected franchises in professional sports. Al lives the Raiders' image but there is a side that is concealed from the public. When his wife suffered a serious stroke, Al stayed for many days by her bedside until she was out of danger. One of the Raiders' administrative staff had a serious stroke and was unconscious in his hospital bed. Al went to the hospital and sat by his side and whispered in his ear that the Raiders would take care of his medical bills, pay his salary and take care of his family while he was sick. Al said, "Just get better." The man recovered and remembered the incident. Davis watches over the Raiders family and is loved and admired by them.

NORBERT EHRENFREUND

Appointed to the San Diego Superior Court Bench in 1978 he still serves in a senior status on the court. Of any judge ever to serve on the San Diego Superior Court he has the most interesting and varied background. He has a distinguished military record serving as an Army Officer in World War II under General George S. Patton in France, Germany and Austria. He received the Bronze Star in the battle of the Rhine. Later he served as a war correspondent for Stars and Strips covering the Nuremberg War Trials.

He received his undergraduate degree from Missouri University and a Masters from Columbia University. Norbert received his law degree, with honors, from Stanford University. He has worked as a reporter for the *Wall Street Journal,* as a producer in television and has had an active career as an actor on the stage. He has served as a prosecutor and help open and was the lead trial attorney for the San Diego Public Defenders Office. Among his many awards and honors he received the Glikbarg Award from Stanford, San Diego Trial Judge of the Year and numerous other awards from the San Diego County Bar Association. He is highly respected by the bench and bar as a thoughtful, intelligent and fair judge.

CHARLES R. FAUST

Born in San Diego, March, 1922, he attended San Diego High School. He served as a bomber pilot in World War II. After the war he went to San Diego State College where he graduated in 1952.

In 1956 he went to work for the San Diego Zoo becoming design director of the Zoo and the Wild Animal Park, retiring in 1990. He is noted for his sand art, drawings and watercolors and is considered by many as one of America's great artists. In 1974 he was honored by San Diego State as Distinguished Alumni and has won hundreds of art awards. The drawings in this work and the *Lifeguards* are original Faust drawings.

He is married 52 years to wife Nancy, and lives in Mission Hills.

HUGO FISHER

Born in San Diego in 1921 he attended San Diego High School, then San Diego State and finally California Western Law School. In 1959 he was elected to the California State Senate. He was defeated in the next election four years later and then appointed by Governor Pat Brown as Secretary of California Resources. In 1963 he was appointed to the San Diego Superior Court where he served until his retirement in 1982. Judge Fisher was considered by lawyers as a fine settlement conference judge. After retiring from the bench he taught Political Science at several colleges. Fisher lives in San Diego and has several adult children.

GENERAL GEORGE W. HICKMAN

General Hickman was acting Dean of the University of San Diego Law School at the time of my graduation. He was referred to as the "General" and was loved and admired by the law students. A Major General in the United States Army he graduated from West Point in 1926, Harvard Law School in 1948 and served as Judge Advocate General of the Army. The General was a principal drafter of the Japanese Peace Treaty. He died several years ago and a scholarship fund was established in his name by his former students.

DEWIT A. (DUTCH) HIGGS

Dutch was admitted to the California Bar in 1934. During World War II he served in the Navy in the Pacific and received the Bronze Star. Dutch was the first person from San Diego to be appointed as a Regent of the University of California where he served for 16 years. He was a President of the San Diego County Bar Association and was the first person from San Diego to serve as President of the California State Bar Association. Dutch was liked and admired by the members of the Bar Association.

J. RICHARD GOODBODY

Known to his friends as "Uncle Rich" he was born in Tombstone, Arizona in 1907 the son of a judge. In 1915 he and his family moved to Coronado where he worked as a paperboy for the San Diego Union-Tribune. In those days the Union had a promotion which gave a year's subscriber a free lot in Imperial Beach. Goodbody was a star football player at Coronado High School. He did his undergraduate studies at the University of California at Berkeley and received his law degree in 1936 from Hastings Law School. In 1943 he was drafted into the Army as a private. Refusing all promotions he was honorably discharged as a private when the war ended.

He was hired as City Attorney for Coronado before the war and remained in that position until 1971. Goodbody was an expert in Municipal, Water and Probate law. "Uncle Rich" died in 1984. His ashes were spread in the water in front of Coronado. He was a great lawyer, a great person and great friend.

WILLIAM T. LOW

Born in Iowa in 1929 his family moved to California that same year. Low received his undergraduate degree from the University of California at Berkeley and his law degree from Hastings Law School in San Francisco. In World War II he served in the Navy and achieved the rank of Captain. He went to work for the San Diego District Attorney and was appointed to the San Diego Municipal Court in 1964 by Governor Pat Brown and elevated to the Superior Court in 1968 by Governor Reagan, where he served with distinction until he retired in 1985. Considered smart and fair he was well-liked by lawyers that appeared before him.

Judge Low lives in La Jolla with his wife; and his son is a respected lawyer in a San Diego civil law defense firm.

WILLIAM P. MAHEDY

Mahedy was born in 1906. He went to Loyola where he obtained his Bachelor's and law degrees. In 1935 he went to work for the San Diego District Attorney. During World War II he served in the United States Navy eventually achieving the rank of Captain. He was appointed to the Superior Court Bench in 1957 by Governor Goodwin Knight where he served for more than 16 years. Known to lawyers as "Wild Bill" he was a colorful attorney, prosecutor and judge.

ARNOLD J. MANDELL

Born in Chicago in 1934 he had a remarkable education. Mandell received his undergraduate degree from Stanford graduating Magna Cum Laude. He received his Medical Degree from Tulane graduating Salutatorian. From 1959 to 1963 he did graduate work at UCLA becoming a specialist in biochemistry and neurochemistry. At 35 he became the youngest person ever to become Chairman of the Department of Psychiatry of a major university in the United States. He has published hundreds of scientific articles, several books and numerous other scholarly works. Mandell is a remarkable person and one of the most interesting persons I have ever met.

JOHN W. MCINNIS

McInnis was born in Brockton, Massachusetts in 1910. He died in San Diego in August 1980. Considered one of the great medical malpractice defense lawyers in California, he was also an officer and the Corporate Lawyer for Pacific Southwest Airlines. He received his Bachelor's and law degrees from Stanford University. During World War II he served as a naval officer in the Pacific. Known to his friends as "Wes" he was President of the San Diego County Bar Association and respected for his many contributions to various charities.

ROBERT MITINGER

Bob was an All-American Football player at Penn State in 1961. He was the first round draft pick of the San Diego Chargers in 1962. While playing for the Chargers he attended the University of San Diego School of Law and graduated in 1965. After football he returned to Pennsylvania where he has a successful law practice in State College. Bob married a San Diego girl, Marilyn, and has two grown daughters.

RONALD J. MIX

Born in Los Angeles in 1938 he attended the University of Southern California where he was an All-American in 1959. Ron was drafted by Baltimore and was also selected as the first round pick to the then Los Angeles Chargers. He played for the Chargers for 10 years and then for two more years for the Raiders. He was an all-pro offensive tackle for nine years and inducted into the Professional Football Hall of Fame in 1979. In addition, he was selected to *Sports Illustrated* All-Time Dream Team. He graduated from the University of San Diego Law School in 1970 and is a respected member of the California Bar Association. Ron referred Paul Low, Houston Ridge and Al Davis to me. His confidence in my ability as a lawyer has meant a lot to me. Married to former Patricia Lanphier since 1965, they have three grown daughters and live in Point Loma.

CHARLES W. REES, JR.

Rees attended Stanford undergraduate and law school graduating from law school in 1959. He is a Fellow in the American College of Trial Lawyers and the American Board of Trial Advocates. He lives in Point Loma with his wife and has five grown children. He is considered by other lawyers and judges as an able, dedicated trial lawyer.

JOHN S. RHOADES

John was born in 1925 and grew up in Laguna Beach, California. He received his BA from Stanford University and his law degree from Hastings Law School in 1951. During World War II he served with distinction in the United States Navy. He practiced law in San Diego in the firm of Rhoades, Hollywood & Neil from 1960 to 1985 when he was appointed by President Ronald Reagan as a Federal District Judge in San Diego. John was highly respected as a trial lawyer and has been a smart and fair District Court Judge. Married to Carmel they have five grown sons.

JOSEPH A. SINCLITICO

Sinclitico was born in Massachusetts in 1915 and departed this world in 1995. He received his undergraduate degree from Holy Cross in 1936, his law degree from Harvard in 1939 and did graduate studies at the University of Chicago and the University of Rome, Del Vecchio.

Joe was admitted to practice law in Pennsylvania, Massachusetts, and Mississippi. In addition he received several honorary degrees. In World War II he served in the United States Army. After the War he began his law teaching career at St. Louis University, Duquesne and Pittsburgh Law Schools. He came to the University of San Diego in 1960 serving as Professor and then Dean of the Law School. After San Diego he helped found the Law School at the University of Puget Sound in Tacoma and taught there from 1972 to 1980. His last teaching assignment was as Distinguished Professor of Law at Mississippi College in Jackson. Throughout his legal career he served as Labor Arbitrator helping resolve hundreds of labor disputes. Joe died in 1995. He is survived by his wife, Grace, and four children, three lawyers and a school teacher. Everyone who knew Joe loved him and is glad he passed through their lives.

CHARLES M. SNELL

Snell was born in 1925 and died in 1995. He served on the San Diego Municipal Court Bench from 1962 until he retired in 1985. During World War II he served in the Army in the Pacific. Chuck was a large, jovial man who was well liked by lawyers.

WILLIAM E. SOMMER

Sommer was born in Chicago in 1919. He attended the University of California at Berkeley graduating in 1940. He served in the Army with distinction in World War II. After the military service he returned to Berkeley where he received his law degree with honors. He practiced law with Higgs, Fletcher & Mack until his appointment to the San Diego Superior Court by Governor Pat Brown in 1965. Bill served with distinction as a trial Judge until retiring in 1977. He and his wife Betty have two grown children and live in La Jolla. The lawyers liked Bill because he was smart, fair and had a fine sense of humor.

DAVID R. THOMPSON

A San Diego native David was born in 1930. He attended Point Loma High School, and received his undergraduate and law degree from the University of Southern California. He served in the Navy from 1955 to 1957 then practiced law with his brother Gordon until Gordon was appointed as a Federal District Court Judge. In 1985 David was appointed as a Judge of the Ninth Circuit Court of Appeals.

David was considered by lawyers as a brilliant trial lawyer and later as an Appellate Judge. Thompson is a charming man who is fair, modest and with a great sense of humor.

He is married to Arna and they have three grown children and still live in Point Loma.

ACKNOWLEDGMENT

My thanks to: Katherine Williams, Kathie Wardrip and
Dan Toporoski who assisted me in editing this work;
Kathleen Blavatt for the book design,
photograph montages and cover art;
Ray Blavatt for his cartoon illustrations;
my lifelong friend Charles R. Faust for his
illustrations and encouragement;
the Frame Station for distributing this work;
and finally, to Dave Marlow of WhitMar Electronic Press
for the excellence of producing this book.

R OBERT BAXLEY a San Diego native, was born in 1929, and was a San Diego City Lifeguard and a Commercial Deep Sea Diver. He went on to practice law in San Diego for many years before being appointed a Judge of the California Superior Court by Governor Pete Wilson. He served with distinction for several years before suffering a serious stroke which forced his retirement. After retiring he wrote his first book *The Lifeguards* which won critical approval by beach goers. Baxley still dives and is a resident in the beach community of Ocean Beach, San Diego, California.

Cover Art by
© Kathleen Blavatt

A publication of the Sunset Cliffs Literary, Poetry and Philosophical Society